CHASING THE ELUSIVE PENNSYLVANIA BIGFOOT

A CRYPTID FROM ANOTHER REALITY

CHASING THE ELUSIVE PENNSYLVANIA BIGFOOT

A CRYPTID FROM ANOTHER REALITY

Paul G. Johnson

Visionary Living Publishing/Visionary Living, Inc.
New Milford, Connecticut

Chasing the Elusive Pennsylvania Bigfoot:
A Cryptid from Another Reality

By Paul G. Johnson

Copyright Paul G. Johnson, 2018

Front cover design by April Slaughter
Back cover and interior design by Leslie McAllister

ISBN: 978-1-942157-29-8 (pbk)
ISBN: 978-1-942157-30-4 (epub)

Published by Visionary Living Publishing/Visionary Living, Inc.
New Milford, Connecticut
www.visionarylivingpublishing.com

TABLE OF CONTENTS

PUBLISHER'S NOTE

In 2016-17, I was researching an essay on Bigfoot for David Weatherly's Volume II of his annual journal, *Wood Knocks*. Brian Seech of the Center for Cryptozoological Studies in Pennsylvania put me in touch with Paul G. Johnson, and I obtained a copy of Johnson's privately published manuscript on his 20-year research of Bigfoot in the Keystone State.

I knew immediately that this work deserved to be brought to a wider audience. Paul's meticulous documentation of his research and analysis of eyewitness accounts and physical evidence is invaluable to all Bigfoot researchers and enthusiasts, regardless of location. In addition, Paul provides a clear discussion of how quantum physics may provide the key to understanding the undeniable para-physical characteristics of this mysterious creature. I persuaded Paul to update his manuscript, which is now released in this book.

Pennsylvania is one of the hottest states in America for Bigfoot activity, with 66 percent of its land covered by forests. Paul has investigated sightings and encounters in the most active zones and has collected an amazing amount of detailed information.

I've been out on some Bigfoot field trips in Pennsylvania, courtesy of Eric H. Altman, another longtime Bigfoot researcher, and who provides a testimonial for this book. I have been out in the field in Washington State with researchers who consider Bigfoot an interdimensional being and not part of the physical "animal world" of our reality. And, I have interviewed many eyewitnesses, including researchers, who observed Bigfoot performing feats and exhibiting characteristics that cannot be explained according to "known laws" of science.

I believe that quantum physics provides the most promising avenue of research to unlocking the secrets of Bigfoot and cannot be overlooked by researchers. How else can we explain how Bigfoot can render itself transparent and invisible, glide rather than walk, instantly relocate itself without walking, pass through solid matter, walk on snow without leaving footprints and suddenly appear and disappear, among other paranormal traits? No creature of the physical world can do those things. A creature that exists in quantum reality can.

Chasing the Elusive Pennsylvania Bigfoot: A Cryptid from an Alternate Reality makes an important contribution to the quantum aspect of Bigfoot research.

– Rosemary Ellen Guiley, Visionary Living Publishing

INTRODUCTION

In 1985, Joan L. Jeffers and I privately published a book entitled *The Pennsylvania Bigfoot*. It chronicled reports of Sasquatch-like creatures sighted by residents in the Keystone State throughout the 1960s, 1970s and early 1980s. The data came from the files of The Pennsylvania Center for UFO Research (PCUFOR). Members of this organization had been investigating Bigfoot reports for many years; Joan Jeffers began her research in 1974. I became involved in creature studies quite by accident.

My introduction to the Sasquatch occurred in 1957 when my cousin and I saw a movie called *The Abominable Snowman of the Himalayas*. I read several books on the subject and decided that perhaps a creature such as this might very well live in the Pacific Northwest or the mountains of Nepal. That Bigfoot might live in Florida, Ohio or Pennsylvania never occurred to me.

In the 1950s, after I saw what I thought was a UFO during a Little League baseball game, I became interested in flying saucers. While in college in 1965, I started a UFO study group in Butler County and continued investigating after moving to Pittsburgh. From 1971-1975, I lived in upstate New York. During this time, a major UFO flap occurred in the eastern United States, and a series of UFO magazines appeared on newsstands. The magazines had names such as *UFO Report*, *Official UFO*, and *Argosy UFO*.

It was in these magazines that articles on Bigfoot began to appear. Several creature sightings were associated with UFOs; other sightings were not. However, these reports were not from northern California and Oregon. The authors of the articles described sightings of giant, hairy, apelike, but upright walking creatures in Indiana, Illinois, Ohio and Pennsylvania. This was my initial introduction to what many people now call the "Eastern Sasquatch." I found the articles interesting but was rather skeptical of the reports.

Joan Jeffers

In 1976, I moved back to Pittsburgh, and in March 1977, I met Joan Jeffers, who was then co-director of PCUFOR. She asked me to join the organization, which had about 75 members at the time. An ex-nurse, Joan was an anthropology student at the University of Pittsburgh. Upon attending the first monthly meeting of the group, I quickly realized that a few members were deeply involved with creature sightings that were occurring in several western Pennsylvania counties. This Bigfoot subculture had existed in PCUFOR for several years, and Joan had investigated a series of creature reports in the north hills section of Pittsburgh. She showed me the plaster casts of several footprints from sighting areas. I must admit they were very large and impressive; however, disappointedly, they did not resemble the print of either man or ape. Although I did not discount the possibility that this mysterious creature did indeed exist in the Keystone State, I initially distanced myself from the research. My main interest was ufology.

Joan finished her studies at Pitt in 1977, and for financial reasons returned to her home in Bradford, Pennsylvania. But Bigfoot sightings continued in the Pittsburgh area, so Joan called me several times and requested that I investigate. For a while I declined, but I finally gave in and began Bigfoot research in the summer of 1977. I quickly realized that the reports of a tall, hairy, bipedal creature roaming about in western Pennsylvania were not hoaxes; nor were they misidentifications of monkeys that escaped from the zoo, or a bear temporarily walking on two legs, as some circus animals do. Much like the UFO phenomenon, I was dealing with credible witnesses reporting sightings of something really incredible, something that had no right to exist.

Our investigations required that we locate witnesses who experienced recent encounters. Each year we sent a Rolodex card with our phone number to every Pennsylvania State Police barracks. There were far too many local police authorities to contact individually, so we sent the cards only to those located in areas where creature sightings often occurred. Along with the card was a letter explaining who we were and what we were trying to accomplish.

Despite our efforts, it is likely that over 90 percent of the sightings went unreported. Why don't witnesses report an encounter with Bigfoot? People who have sightings normally have no prior knowledge or interest in the phenomenon. They might expect to see Bigfoot when visiting Mount St. Helens in Washington State, but not while picnicking in Westmoreland County. Therefore, they are not aware that sightings often occur in the eastern United States, and that there are organizations with hotline numbers that investigate reports.

Articles on our group appeared often in newspapers, but most people ignored them for the same reason I skip the "Food" section of the Sunday *Post Gazette.* I have no interest in cooking. Occasionally, Pennsylvania residents may read an article on Sasquatch; however, their responses are skepticism or even downright disdain. And surely, they don't record the hotline number in their address books with the expectation of a future encounter.

A few witnesses possess the intellect to realize they have observed something important and profound, something that could very well change our understanding of biology as we know it. These people immediately find a way of reporting their experiences. Acquiring a sighting report at the time it happens would enable an investigator not only to interview the witness but also to examine the sighting area for the physical trace evidence that should still be present. However, this seldom happens. Normally, the Center receives the report weeks or months or sometimes even years after the sighting. This necessitates gathering evidence by probing the memories of the witnesses.

In 1977, my area of expertise was flying saucers. I had no knowledge of the history of the Sasquatch. By 1984, Joan and I had investigated a number of reports, but I didn't know what to do with them. To sort things out, we sat down and put together all our research results. This generated a manuscript that evolved into the book we published in 1985. Our investigations continued into the next decade. We set up an 800 hotline number where police and ordinary citizens could report Bigfoot and UFO sightings.

Creature reports came in from many areas of Pennsylvania. Our research continued until the untimely death of Joan Jeffers in 1998. By then, the internet was popular, and dozens of Bigfoot websites began to appear.

Around this time, two young investigators started the Pennsylvania Bigfoot Society (PBS). The organization grew over the years, and its members did an excellent job investigating creature sightings in the Keystone State. As a PBS member, I was occasionally asked to investigate several sightings. A few of these appear in this book.

I would like to extend my appreciation to Eric H. Altman, the former director of the PBS, and to Brian Seech and Fred Saluga for keeping me in the loop with respect to recent creature and UFO activity in Pennsylvania. Brian and his wife, Terri, are especially interested in cryptid reports from western Pennsylvania and eastern Ohio. They can be contacted at centerforcryptostudies@yahoo.com.

The investigator who started PCUFOR in the early 1970s is Stan Gordon. He has written an excellent book entitled *Silent Invasion: The Pennsylvania UFO-Bigfoot Casebook*. He can be contacted at paufo@comcast.net.

CHAPTER 1

THE LEGEND OF SLEEPY HOLLOW

In doing investigations of any kind, it seems that after a period of time, a witness or a clue appears that completely changes the direction of the research. This happened to me at 11:20 AM on 20 December 1988. I had just finished recording the final grades of my 300 students in the college chemistry course I was teaching when the phone rang. The voice of an elderly man on the other end asked me if I was the Dr. Johnson at Duquesne University who investigated Bigfoot sightings. After asserting that I was, he told me his name was Samuel J. Sherry, Jr. and asked if l would like to hear about a sighting he had the previous May in Westmoreland County. I eagerly said yes and grabbed my pen and notebook. However, he didn't care to talk on the phone. He wanted me to drive to his house near Ligonier.

I suspected a hoax and tried asking the witness several questions about his sighting, but he evaded answering them. He was insistent on meeting me in person. Luckily, my semester had just ended, and although it was rather cold outside, no snow was predicted, so I arranged to meet him later that afternoon. Normally, I would take another investigator on trips such as this; however, everyone I called was too busy preparing for the Christmas holiday. I grabbed the camera from my desk drawer, walked to the parking garage, jumped into my pickup truck and headed east on the parkway toward the Squirrel Hill tunnels.

Per Sam Sherry's directions, I took the Lincoln Highway east to Ligonier before turning north on Route 711. Two miles later, I reached Oak Grove where I made a left turn and headed toward the village of Wilpen. Arriving there, I pulled into a yard next to a mailbox with the name Samuel J. Sherry. As I climbed from my truck, I noticed the telltale odor of burning coal in the chilly air. The aroma was familiar because my parents heated our home with coal throughout the 1950s.

I knocked on the door of the small, wood-framed home and was welcomed by Sam and his wife. Little did I know, but this was a trip I would make hundreds of times for the next 15 years as Sam and I later investigated dozens of Bigfoot sightings in Westmoreland and Somerset Counties.

On this particular December day, I sat at their kitchen table, and Mrs. Sherry poured me a cup of freshly brewed coffee. Then Sam began telling me about his encounter. He said he often went lantern fishing after dark on the Loyalhanna Creek. Trout was his favorite catch.

On the evening of 17 May 1988, he drove across the causeway at Sleepy Hollow and parked his blue 1975 Maverick on the south side of the creek. As usual, the witness climbed from his car and retrieved the fishing paraphernalia in the trunk. He was carrying a flashlight and casually glanced at his watch. The time was exactly 11:30 PM.

It was then that Sam noticed a musty odor like "foul damp air" in the area. He compared it to the smell of a wet dog or the stale smell often found in damp, underground cellars.

Sleepy Hollow Causeway. The road to the left leads to Route 30 east.

Sam heard strange noises coming from a wooded area below the eastbound lane of Route 30. "I heard this loud commotion," he said. "There were shrill whistling, grunting, and monkey-like chattering sounds coming out of the woods." There were also other recognizable noises such as branches being broken and animals walking and stumbling. Sam shined his flashlight toward the area and saw glowing orange eyes, but little else.

Then at the edge of the woods, about 20 feet away, appeared a tall, bipedal creature. Sam was shocked because he did not see the figure walk from the woods to where it stood. It was just suddenly there. He estimated that the strange figure was one or two inches shy of being seven feet in height.

Sam first noticed the creature's head. It was large, but not out of proportion to the remainder of the body. The witness estimated that the head was larger than a soccer ball but smaller than a basketball. The two

This is a sketch of the creature observed at the Sleepy Hollow causeway on 17 May 1988. It was drawn by one of our investigators based on a description provided her by Sam Sherry.

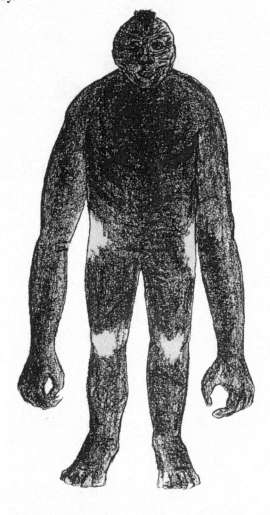

The Sleepy Hollow Bigfoot witnessed by Sam Sherry.

eyes were the size of golf balls and exhibited orange eyeshine. No pupil or iris was discernible; however, when illuminated, the eyes appeared to constrict, as if they were trying to refocus.

The face was "deeply wrinkled and had a leather-like appearance." The facial skin seemed to have a reddish-brown tone, as did the rest of the body. The creature had two ears, but they were small and flush with the head. The nose was flattened against the face, exposing two large nares. The top of the head was bare except for a two-inch high, and two-inch wide swath of hair that began at the top of the forehead and extended to the lower back of the head. This gave the creature the appearance of having a Mohawk-style haircut. All of the hair was very well kept, as if it were being constantly preened. On each side of the head was a horseshoe-shaped segment of hair that originated below the ears and terminated below the eyes.

The creature had no neck. The shoulders were broad and the remaining torso long and indistinct. The creature possessed no discernible waist, hips, buttocks or genitalia. It had two legs that ended in rather human-looking feet that the witness described as not being extraordinarily large considering the creature's size and weight. Each foot had five toes.

The creature's arms were very long, hanging well below the knees while standing erect. It had two very large hands, each with four fingers and an opposable thumb. The fingers did not appear to have any claws or nails. There was no hair on the arms, hands, legs, feet or torso. The reddish-brown skin was leathery-like, and well worn.

"It was as if this thing was always scratching itself, and that's why the skin and fingernails were so worn," said Sam. Areas on the shoulders, elbows and knees were especially deteriorated.

There were also a number of gray patches of skin on the knees and torso, as if the creature had a mange-like disease. Sam guessed this creature was very, very old. When initially observed, it "stood perfectly erect" with its arms at its side. It was not bent at its shoulders or hips. The witness noticed it was breathing loudly and heavily as if it had an asthmatic condition. The creature continually spit saliva as it wheezed. Its mouth was puckered, an effect the witness thought was due to the creature's unusual breathing pattern. According to Sam, it "appeared to suck in more air than it breathed out." After a minute or so, it finally expelled the pent-up gas in one heavy, long exhalation.

Then the creature started acting in a challenging manner. It began swinging its arms, followed by beating its chest, and finally by flexing its muscles. Sam felt there were other creatures still in the woods, and this one was putting on a display in defense of the others. After several minutes, it discontinued the display.

"I wasn't scared at all," he reported. "My instincts told me this thing wasn't going to harm me. I've been hunting and fishing for years, and my instincts have always told me whether an animal is dangerous or not."

Sam turned his back on the creature and calmly walked to the front door of his Maverick. Suddenly, it was there next to him. He didn't hear any footfalls, which gave him the impression it moved much too fast to have merely walked or run. The creature brushed up against Sam's elbow and fingered his jacket. Sam climbed into his car and closed the door. The creature put its hands on the open window.

"The pressure of its weight pressed the car down," said Sam. "So, I said, 'Listen, Biggie, you're going to bust my tires if you don't stop that.' Then it leaned its head through the open window and spit all over me as it wheezed."

He said it had "terrible breath odor" that he likened to "spoiled seafood." "Its head was only two feet from mine, and he slobbered all over my face. I didn't try to wipe the spit off. I was afraid to touch

Rough Sketch of Loyalhanna Gorge Area (Not to Scale)

---- = Loyalhanna River

217 north to Derry

W

Route 30 West

Kingston
Dam

culvert underneath
Route 30

x

causeway

Chestnut Ridge

Stream flowing
from St. Clair
Hollow into
Loyalhanna R.

E

Route 30 East

St. Clair Hollow

Route 30

Chestnut Ridge

Longbridge

Loyalhanna River

Flowing from East to West, the Loyalhanna River cuts a narrow gorge through the Chestnut Ridge. Route 30 east and weat are separated in this area. Sleepy Hollow provides a causeway where vehicles can cross over the other direction. X marks the spot where Sam Sherry parked his car on the evening of 17 May 1988.

it." Sam started the car and drove away. As he did so, he noticed that creature had not moved. It stood there with its right arm stretched out as if saying goodbye.

For years, this particular section of the Loyalhanna has been referred to as Sleepy Hollow. Sam Sherry had been lantern fishing in the area many times in the past. Sleepy Hollow is also a place where young people hang out throughout the summer. On this particular evening, the causeway was unusually quiet. There were no people and no apparent traffic on Route 30. He didn't recall hearing the usually rapid-flowing creek. During the approximate 20-minute duration of the sighting, no vehicles exited Route 30 and crossed the causeway.

One of the first steps in the analysis of a creature sighting is to consider the possibility of a hoax perpetrated by the witness. This was especially important here because the close encounter was very strange and highly different from other Bigfoot sightings I investigated.

Sam Sherry and his wife, Naomi, owned their one-story frame house in Wilpen. In the early 1900s, this village was home to hundreds of immigrants from Central Europe, who worked in nearby coal mines. Sam's father, Steven, arrived from Hungary around 1912 and became a coal miner. He later married, built the home in Wilpen, and had four children, two girls and two boys.

According to the 1930 U.S. Population Census, "Sammy" was born in 1922 and was the third oldest sibling. As a teenager, he was drafted into the army and fought the Japanese in the South Pacific during World War II. He was severely wounded and remained in a coma for months. After more than a year of slow recovery in the hospital, he returned to his family home in Wilpen and married Naomi. They had two children. Naomi regularly attended the Orthodox Church in Wilpen, where she was also a part-time caretaker.

Naomi asserts that before this incident, Sam had never talked about Bigfoot. He is an avid reader, but she cannot recall him buying or borrowing any material dealing with Bigfoot or UFOs. She claims

Sam Sherry at site of Sleepy Hollow Bigfoot encounter on March 23, 1989.

he came home early that evening, and there was a strange odor on his clothing. He immediately bathed. He did not tell his wife about the encounter. Sam claimed he was confused and embarrassed. He did not feel anyone would believe him. Only later did he discover there were people in Pennsylvania who investigated these unusual reports.

Over a period of time, I met and interviewed several people who had known Sam for years. Robert Colt owned Windy Hill Farm, where he raised horses. He had been a neighbor of the Sherry family for decades. Sam always referred to his neighbor as Mr. Colt, and I began to do the same. When I first interviewed Mr. Colt, he verified that Sam had never mentioned the topic of Bigfoot over the years. They talked only about hunting and fishing.

Mr. Colt was an ex-game warden and an expert marksman with the bow and arrow, as well as a musket. Subsequently, he occasionally would accompany Sam and me as we searched for Bigfoot. Although he was open-minded, Mr. Colt was skeptical that such an animal could exist. However, he sincerely vouched for Sam's veracity with respect to the topic.

Over the years, I listened to Sam Sherry describe his encounter to several Bigfoot investigators and reporters. That his story was not rehearsed was quite apparent. Each time it was a little different, but not in the most important aspects of the case. Yes, he did tend to embellish slightly, but that is to be expected from someone who slowly realized he had a very special and very strange encounter that few other people would ever experience in their lifetime.

The Borough of Ligonier is about 60 miles east of Pittsburgh. It draws its name from a fort constructed by a Colonel Bouquet in 1758 and named for Sir John Ligonier, commander-in-chief of the English army. It served as a supply depot between Fort Bedford and Fort Pitt during the French and Indian War. The fort was located in the Ligonier Valley, a long corridor that runs north to south between the Chestnut Ridge to its west and the Laurel Mountain to its east. Ligonier became prominent as a settlement because it also happens to be located in the Loyalhanna Gorge that bisects the Chestnut Ridge in the east-west direction where Route 30 now stands.

The area surrounding Ligonier contained a number of Indian trails, and at one time an Indian settlement called "Loyalhannon" existed there. In 1763, there was an Indian uprising, and on 3 June 1763, the English successfully defended the fort against an attack. In the 1790s, Pennsylvania constructed the east-west road that passed through Ligonier, and the village began to grow. In the early 1800s, the Harrisburg-Pittsburgh Turnpike replaced the older road and stagecoach travel began. Inns opened as small villages along the road prospered, and Ligonier was no exception. In 1834, with about 300 inhabitants, it became a borough.

Sleepy Hollow lies in the aforementioned Loyalhanna Gorge. It is situated where a stream from St. Clair Hollow flows into the Loyalhanna River. It was named after General Arthur St. Clair (1736-1818), who built a grist mill on his estate in the hollow.

After my initial interview with Sam, we drove to the sighting area where he re-enacted the event in its entirety. Even though his encounter was over six months old, I spent hours looking for footprints or other physical traces suggesting that a creature of this sort was visiting the area. All I found were deer tracks and one dead squirrel.

I returned home and waited for some snow, hoping I might find tracks in Sleepy Hollow. Returning on 21 January 1989, I walked along the causeway and part way up St. Clair Hollow. Only raccoon and deer prints were easily visible. On 27 January, I returned to Wilpen to finalize my report by asking Sam a few more questions. He told me he heard about a Bigfoot sighting in Blairsville Cemetery, but did not know the name of the witness.

He also told me about "the birdman." This was a name several people had given to a Westmoreland County resident named Bob, who had an encounter with Bigfoot near Gray Station in Derry Township sometime in 1986.

Apparently, Bob raised parakeets in a trailer he shared with his wife. According to Sam, the creature picked up a piece of wood and threw it at the witness. Sam and I spent several months trying to track down the birdman. All we knew was that he lived in a trailer outside of Latrobe. So, I began visiting trailer parks.

11

CHAPTER 2

TORNADOES AND BIGFOOT LOVE
TRAILER COURTS

On 4 March 1989, I stopped at a trailer park that sits at the end of a dirt road just outside of Gray Station. One of the residents told me I was in the right park and pointed out the birdman's trailer. No one answered my knock on the door. It was a windy, 60-degree Saturday, so I sat in my truck and waited for Bob to return.

After five hours, I drove over the ridge to Sam's house. He was not home, so I told Naomi to tell him I found the trailer. I returned to Gray Station several times over the next few weeks before another resident told me Bob was in the process of moving to Armaugh, in Indiana County, and that was why he was seldom there.

Finally, on Good Friday, 24 March 1989, the birdman drove his station wagon into the trailer court outside of Gray Station. He was a bit apprehensive as I approached, but his demeanor eased when he realized I was just a Bigfoot investigator. He and his wife invited me into their trailer, which was nearly empty, as they had moved most of their furniture to Armaugh. I relaxed in a small chair, notebook in hand, while the birdman related his encounter that occurred along the railroad tracks just a few hundred yards from where I sat.

Deer season is probably the most highly anticipated and important event in rural western Pennsylvania. In 1986, the three days allocated for hunting antlered deer began on 11 December and terminated at sunset on the 13th. Late on the last day, Bob left the woods and walked to the Conrail Railroad bed between Torrance and Gray Station. He proceeded to walk the tracks toward his home in the trailer park. Suddenly an object fell at his feet. He thought it was a log. He looked up to see a strange, hairy, bipedal creature standing on the railroad bed about 100 yards away. The figure's left arm was lowering to its side, giving Bob the impression that this "thing" had thrown the object, presumably to attract his attention.

The creature was apelike, except it stood erect on two legs. It was between seven and eight feet tall and had long, black hair. "I could see the long hair on its arms," remarked Bob. "It stood there with its head cocked, just staring at me. And I just stared back. I raised the rifle to my chest, but no further. It looked too human to me, and it was big, at least three times the size of a man. It had broad shoulders, very, very broad shoulders. I was scared at first, but I needed to get by him to go back to my trailer. So I stood my ground. We must have stared at each other for several minutes."

The glare from the setting sun made seeing detail difficult. However, Bob did notice that it had large red eyes and a huge head that appeared to sit directly on those broad shoulders. The head came to a point at the top and was completely covered with hair. He noticed that the arms were long, hanging slightly below the knees.

After several more minutes, the creature turned and walked down the tracks away from the witness and toward Gray Station. Then it suddenly veered to the left and ran into the woods. It took tremendously long strides, and Bob could hear the creature breathing heavily, "as if it had asthma."

As Bob continued to walk down the tracks toward home, he noticed an uncomfortable, sulfur odor permeating the area. At home, his parakeets were unusually restless, banging against their cages as if trying to get out. Bob slept restlessly that night.

Gray Station is a small village located in Derry Township, Westmoreland County. The township was established in 1775 and is a wide valley bound on the north by the Conemaugh River, the east by the crest of the Chestnut Ridge, and the south by the Loyalhanna Creek. According to a county history (John N. Boucher, *Old and New Westmoreland*, Vol. 1, The American Historical Society, 1918), the original settlers were annoyed by Indian and wild animal incursions. The following quote from the book seemed appropriate at the time I was investigating reports.

> *At night these animals [bears] made hideous sounds as they prowled around homesteads in search of domestic animals, so that the country was then literally a "howling wilderness." There was no howl more dismal to an early settler and his family than a howling wolf, unless it was the bloodcurdling cry of an Indian, which was often heard by the early inhabitants of Derry Township.*

In the 1850s, the Pennsylvania Railroad mainline was built and ran along the base of the Chestnut Ridge through Derry, Millwood, Hillside and Torrance before crossing the Conemaugh River into Indiana County. Gray Station was the smallest village along the line. It was, and even now, sometimes referred to as Gray Crossing by the locals. There are fewer than three dozen homes in the community. Limestone mining was active on the ridge for decades, and remnants of the tram used to move the stone to the railroad crossing still remain.

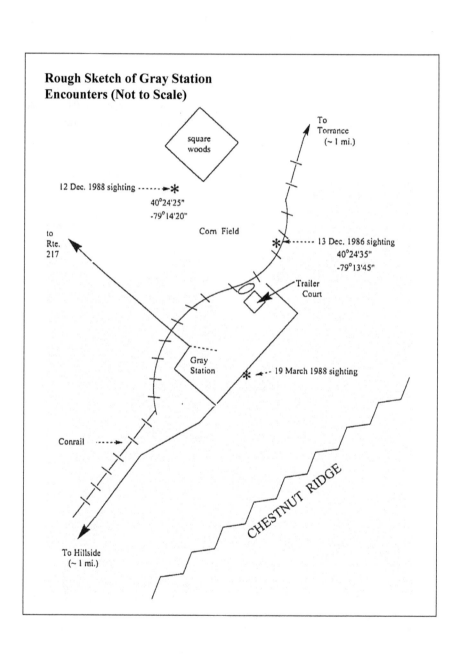

Rough Sketch of Gray Station Encounters (Not to Scale)

square woods

To Torrance (~ 1 mi.)

12 Dec. 1988 sighting ------▶✳
40°24'25"
-79°14'20"

to Rte. 217

Corn Field

✳------ 13 Dec. 1986 sighting
40°24'35"
-79°13'45"

Trailer Court

Gray Station

✳◀--- 19 March 1988 sighting

Conrail ----▶

CHESTNUT RIDGE

To Hillside (~ 1 mi.)

The birdman had two more encounters with Bigfoot, both occurring two years later, in 1988. On 19 March, Bob was driving along the back road to his home near Gray Station between 12:45 and 1 AM. The night was particularly dark, and he was alone in his station wagon. At the bottom of a steep grade, two deer suddenly ran from the right side of the road into a wooded area on the left. Then a tall, erect-walking, hairy, apelike creature did the same and disappeared into the darkness. He saw the creature in profile for only a few seconds but was still able to discern glowing red eyes. It was seven to eight feet tall, with long, black hair, and arms reaching below the knees. He stopped, rolled down his windows, and noticed a musty odor lingering in the night air. He then nervously drove home.

Bob and a friend were hunting in a cornfield near Gray Station, less than one mile west of the railroad tracks, on 12 December 1988. This first day of deer season was cold in Western Pennsylvania. It was 12 degrees Fahrenheit and there was snow on the ground. A number of hunters were within view. Bob's friend first saw the movement. He noticed that the arms were long, hanging slightly below the knees. After several minutes, the creature turned and walked down the tracks, away from the witness and toward Gray Station. Like the creature seen by Bob in 1986, it took tremendously long strides, and the witness heard the creature breathing heavily, "as if it had asthma."

Upon raising his rifle and looking through the scope, Bob saw an apelike creature walking along the edge of a wooded area. It was very tall with long, black hair over its entire body. The witness could see its breath condensing in front of its face as it walked swiftly towards another wooded area.

"Even through the scope I couldn't see much of the face," said Bob. "It was too dark-colored. I saw that it had two large breasts, making me think it was a female."

Apparently, the creature's face, although not completely hair-covered, had black skin, which made it difficult to discern detail at a distance. Also, it was several hundred yards away. The head was large and came to a point on the top.

17

Rough Diagram of Towns and Villages on the Western Base of the Chestnut Ridge (Not to Scale)

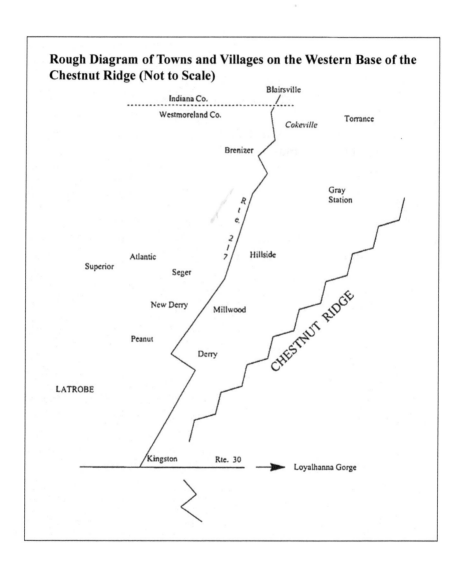

Bob and his friend watched the figure walk until it disappeared into an area the locals called the "square woods." The witnesses later found a three-toed print in the snow where the creature had walked. Also, a light, musty odor lingered in the area. I contacted Bob's companion, who verified the report but did not want to be interviewed.

After spending time with the birdman on several occasions, I found no evidence of deception on his part. I talked separately to three of his neighbors who told me they never had any indications that Bob fabricated stories. Despite goodnatured kidding from several of his friends, the witness has never retracted any of his statements. Of course, I was initially suspicious because he reported seeing the creature on three different occasions. However, as I was soon to learn, several sightings are not unusual in the cryptozoology field.

More Westmoreland County sightings

The date was 1 May 1989, and I was finalizing my investigations on the Gray Station encounters when the phone rang. The caller introduced herself as Beth, and she wanted to know if I was interested in older Bigfoot sightings from Westmoreland County. After I told her yes, she informed me that her family had a series of encounters in a trailer park near the small village of Superior during the summer of 1973. I was vaguely aware of these reports from newspaper clippings in the files I inherited from the Pennsylvania Center for UFO Research. The files contained dozens of creature reports and several UFO sightings that occurred in 1973. Beth and I arranged to meet the following weekend at her home, which was now located near Brenizer, not far from Gray Station.

As I sat in her living room, Beth told me about a series of encounters she and her family experienced in 1973. Beth and her husband, Carl, sat at the kitchen table in their trailer on a warm summer evening around11:30 PM. Looking out the window, they saw the back of a seven-to-eight feet tall, hairy, apelike creature walking through the trailer park. It had brown hair over its entire body and long arms that hung well below the knees. The head was very large and appeared to be somewhat pointed on top. The witnesses never saw the face. The creature

19

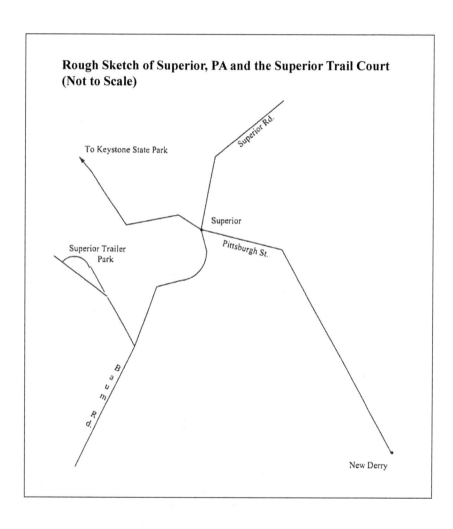

Rough Sketch of Superior, PA and the Superior Trail Court (Not to Scale)

Superior Rd.

To Keystone State Park

Superior

Superior Trailer Park

Pittsburgh St.

B a u m R d.

New Derry

was stocky and walked in a "lumbering way." It ultimately disappeared into the darkness. No odors or sounds were noticed. A neighbor later told Beth that she also saw the profile of the same creature that night as it walked through the court.

Interestingly, about 30 minutes before the sighting, Beth's three-year-old daughter began screaming. She told her parents that she woke up and saw a man with an orange-colored glow looking in her bedroom window.

Several days later, Beth, her daughter, and her cousin were walking through a wooded area near their trailer court when they saw a tall, hairy, erect-walking biped ambling toward them. Beth told her cousin to take the daughter and run while she ran in the other direction, hoping the creature would follow her. Within a few seconds, the creature turned and walked deeper into the woods. Beth said it resembled the one she saw previously walking through the trailer court. It had dark brown hair, long arms, and a pointed head. There was not sufficient light to discern facial details. The creature made no noise, but the witness did detect a "sulfur odor" in the area. She also noted, as in the previous sighting, that the creature exhibited a lumbering gait.

Beth's next encounter that summer gave her by far the best look at the creature. She had left her trailer to walk next door to use the neighbor's telephone. As she knocked on the door, a tall, hairy biped walked out of the woods and stepped onto a bank about 10 feet away. The creature stood there glaring at the witness. Beth froze but then recovered enough to scream. The creature raised its arms as though attempting to cover both ears. The figure finally turned and retreated to the woods. The witness ran in the opposite direction.

Again, she estimated the creature was between seven to eight feet tall, with brown fur covering its entire body. Its hands were large with long, hair-covered fingers. The face "appeared to be something halfway between a man and an ape," but it was not completely hair-covered. The nose was large and wide. The eyes were the size of half dollars and reflected an amber color. Beth could not recall details concerning the mouth and ears. As in the previous sighting, she noticed a sulfur-like odor.

On a warm summer evening in 1973, while doing her laundry, Beth's neighbor opened the back door of her trailer to shake the feathers from a pillow case before putting it into the washer. About 20 feet away, she saw a seven-foot tall, apelike creature standing on two legs and staring at her. It had brownish-black hair and stood perfectly erect. The head was large and round on top. It had hair on its face, but the only other facial detail she could recollect were the red eyes. They stood and looked at each other for several seconds before the creature turned and hurried away. The witness screamed and slammed the door.

These sightings from 1973 exemplify behavior patterns often associated with the Pennsylvania Bigfoot. The creature appears to be rather curious in some cases and completely indifferent to human presence in others. Trailer parks are easy targets for curious animals; all human activity is on one floor, close to the ground, and easily observable. Overall, the creature is non-aggressive, retreating shortly after human contact.

I tried to locate other residents of the trailer court from names provided by Beth; however, they had moved away within the 16-year period. One of the witnesses, the woman who was doing her laundry when she encountered the creature, had moved to Derry. I stopped at her home several times during June 1989, but no one was ever home. A neighbor later informed me the woman had moved. I was never able to locate a new address.

CHAPTER 3

That Which Was But Is No More

From 1970-2000, Westmoreland County provided the most Bigfoot activity in Pennsylvania. Although the county is quite large, most of the sightings centered on and around the Chestnut Ridge. Sightings on the Laurel Mountain and areas in Somerset County just to the east of the Chestnut do occur, as one can see in the chronological listing of reports at the end of this manuscript; however, they are minimal. Also, for some unknown reason, the large majority of sightings occur around the small villages that dot the western base of the Chestnut Ridge, such as Derry, Gray Station, Brenizer and Torrance. This pattern continued into the 1990s. Note that all of the birdman's sightings occurred on the western base of the ridge.

Between Christmas 1988 and New Year's Day, I stopped at the office of a local newspaper, *The Blairsville Dispatch*, and placed an advertisement in the personals column concerning my research on Bigfoot. Blairsville sits on the Indiana County side of the Conemaugh

River. A month later, I received a call from a man who resided in Brenizer. He related the sighting of a hairy creature earlier in January 1989 in the village of Cokeville, not far from his house. I made an appointment to meet the witness at his home the following weekend. After hanging up, I spent an hour looking through my Westmoreland County maps for the town of Cokeville, to no avail. I concluded that the phone call was a hoax; however, I planned to look for tracks on the Chestnut Ridge that weekend, anyway, so I stopped at the address given to me by the witness. Surprisingly, he was home.

Then I discovered Cokeville was a ghost town. It was originally called Broad Fording because it was the only area where a Westmoreland County resident could ford the Conemaugh River to access Blairsville. The village and its environs comprised about 300 acres. Around 1872, the Isabella Furnace Company purchased land just outside of Broad Fording and constructed 100 beehive coke ovens. After this, the village became known as Cokeville. A bridge was built in 1886 connecting Cokeville with Blairsville, but it was subsequently destroyed by a tornado. A second one was built but was washed away by the Johnstown flood in 1889. A third bridge was constructed and lasted until it was destroyed by the flood on St. Patrick's Day, 1936. The coke ovens operated until the early 1900s before closing.

In 1952, Cokeville became the victim of the Conemaugh River Flood Control Project. The federal government purchased all the homes and farms, forcing the residents to vacate the village. The entire area was razed in anticipation of its ultimate flooding. However, except for a few wetlands, most of what was Cokeville is still above water.

After picking up the witness in Brenizer, I parked along Route 217. We squeezed through a gate and strolled down a macadam road that used to be Route 680, toward Cokeville. As we walked along, to our left was a steep hillside that once provided openings to coal mines. The openings were now bricked shut and covered with vines. To the right was a wetlands. Knowing that along these roads were homes subsequently abandoned by people who really didn't want to leave gave me an eerie feeling. I thought perhaps a creature such as Bigfoot might

24

remain secluded here. The area was off limits to vehicular traffic and free of inhabitants. Little did I know that I was soon to receive more creature reports from other ghost towns in Westmoreland County.

After walking for about one-half mile, we reached the area where the witness had his sighting. Back in early January, he was walking toward McGee Run to check on some traps he had set several days earlier. Around dawn, he saw a figure about six feet tall walk down a hillside in a "strange loping manner." The creature was partially hidden by brush, but as it walked diagonally, it came within about 60 feet of the witness before disappearing into a clump of trees.

At that distance, the witness was able to observe that the figure was not a man, but instead an apelike creature whose hair-covered head bobbed in an unusual manner as it lumbered out of sight. It was not light enough for the witness to discern other features.

The sighting occurred near an air-vent to an old coal mine, and the witness theorized that the biped might be using the vent to access the mine. He claimed to have observed a hairy creature twice before, once in the summer of 1967, and again in 1968. In both cases, he said that "it sounded like a bulldozer as it ran through the weeds." Both sightings were at the base of the Chestnut Ridge.

This is an example of an aspect of the Bigfoot phenomenon that repeated itself many times over the years. Most people have never seen one Bigfoot, myself included. But in many instances, those few who reported a sighting to our Center also had experienced an earlier encounter or had subsequent encounters.

After leaving the witness, I drove across the ridge to visit Sam Sherry. He was interested in looking at the area, so we returned to Cokeville the following weekend. It was February 1989, but still warm enough to spend some time in the woods. The ravine that housed the air-vent was filled with old tires and other junk people had thrown into the valley from the hillside above.

Sam climbed down a small embankment into the air-vent. He found only deer and dog tracks around the vent. The opening was less than 10 feet long and much too small for a man to actually access the mine. It would have been impossible for the hairy creature observed in January to enter the mine through this vent. We spent the remainder of the day exploring Cokeville and its environs. Since this was a government-controlled wetlands, and not private property, we were free to roam without fear of trespassing. Only motorized vehicles were prohibited. We were even able to locate a few of the old beehive coke ovens. The ground was wet and soft, and we walked for miles. However, the only tracks we found were from deer and a variety of small animals.

This was not to be my only experience with ghost towns and flood control areas. Over the years, I heard rumors of creature sightings in Livermore, another ex-village that sat on the Conemaugh River in Derry Township, a few miles west of Blairsville. Most of the reports were second- and third-hand, so I was unable to investigate them in detail. According to history books, the streets of Livermore were laid out in 1827 by a John Livermore, who named the village after himself. It gained importance because the Pennsylvania Canal passed through the town, and it ultimately became a stop on the Western Pennsylvania Railroad. In 1865, Livermore became a borough. For years, the village and the surrounding area often flooded when the Conemaugh overflowed. As in the case of Cokeville, this prompted the federal government to buy the land, move the people out and dismantle the town. What was once Livermore is now principally under water. All that remains are the old railroad beds and tunnels.

I did receive the report of a creature sighted around June 1959 in Livermore. Not long after graduating from Saltsburg High School, a woman and her boyfriend were sitting on the Indiana County side of the Conemaugh. Around dusk, they decided to return to his Nash Rambler parked along one of the flood control roads. As they approached the front of the car, the woman observed a seven-foot tall, hairy creature with an apelike face slowly walking toward them along the road. The creature was covered with dark black hair and "walked perfectly erect just like a man does." It did not appear to be in any particular hurry.

The witness stated, "We jumped into the car and guess what? It wouldn't start! Just like in the movies. But it finally started just as this thing reached our trunk, and my boyfriend sped out of there. That area was a typical place for Saltsburg kids to park. But we never went back there. And we never told anybody about seeing this thing."

My first trip to Livermore occurred on 17 July 1990. Earlier in the day, I had driven to Somerset, Pennsylvania to place an advertisement in *The Daily American* because I had heard about possible creature sightings in the area. Upon returning west on Route 22, I stopped in Cokeville and unsuccessfully looked for tracks under the Torrance Bridge. It was only 3 PM, so I decided to visit Livermore. I had never been there before but had received vague directions in a letter from a man who suggested that others had seen Bigfoot in the wetlands. In the letter, the man told me not to go there alone unless I was armed, because packs of wild dogs reportedly roamed the marshes. However, I was alone, and I never pack. After driving two or three miles north from Route 22, I crossed a set of railroad tracks and traveled another one-quarter mile where the road ended at a chained gate. On the other side of the gate was a hill that went down to the old railroad bed near where the Livermore passenger station was once located. I spent several hours taking pictures as I walked the viaduct.

Upon returning to my vehicle, I noticed the sign marking the entrance to the Livermore Cemetery, which sits high on a hill above the Conemaugh. For several years, the cemetery was rumored to be haunted, and young kids often used the grounds for beer drinking. Apparently, this recently resulted in vandalism of the cemetery, so that now no trespassing signs are posted.

It was not so on this hot July evening in 1990, so I walked to the top of the road and stepped into the small cemetery. Surprisingly, as I walked around the edge of the ground near the rim of the hill overlooking the Conemaugh, I found a series of what appeared to be footprints. One set was only about 10 inches long; however, I located a second set that was 18 inches long, four inches wide at the heel, and seven inches wide in front. The prints appeared to have toes; however, they were difficult to

Rough Sketch of Livermore Area in 1991 (Not to Scale)

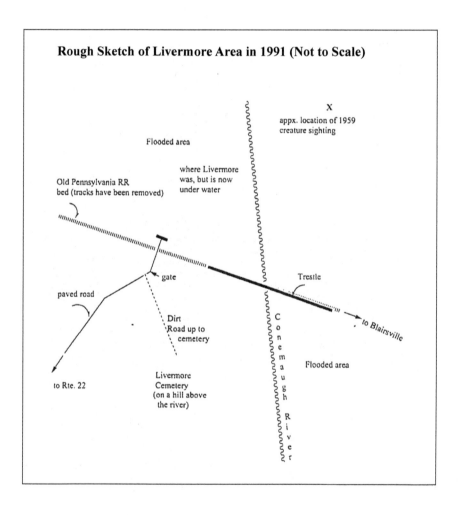

X
appx. location of 1959
creature sighting

Flooded area

where Livermore
was, but is now
under water

Old Pennsylvania RR
bed (tracks have been removed)

gate

paved road

Trestle

to Blairsville

Dirt
Road up to
cemetery

Conemaugh River

Flooded area

to Rte. 22

Livermore
Cemetery
(on a hill above
the river)

discern because the area was grassy. Dusk was approaching, so I drove back to Route 22 and headed home.

On July 19, I returned with plaster of Paris and made molds of some of the prints. After extracting the molds from the ground and removing the dirt, I examined them. Upon closer inspection, I decided they were not footprints but were caused by something else. The imprints were most likely generated by the tractor used to mow the lawn in the cemetery.

In 1993, my attention was drawn to a connection between Bigfoot and ghost towns. This time, however, the location was east of the Chestnut Ridge in Indiana County and did not involve flood control projects. The sighting occurred in an old mining town.

Throughout the late 19th and early 20th centuries, coal mining was the principal industry in Indiana County. As mines began to open, settlements grew nearby. One of these was Claghorn in Brush Valley Township where Brush Valley Creek flows into Blacklick Creek. Partway between Homer City and Armaugh, Claghorn was founded in 1903 and named after Clarence Raymond Claghorn, superintendent of the Lackawanna Coal and Coke Company. In the early 1900s, the village had 80 homes, a company store, a hotel with 22 rooms, a movie theater, and a schoolhouse. At one time, nearly 1,000 men, women and children lived in the town. People began moving away in 1923 when mining coal in the area became unprofitable. By 1930, only 270 people remained. By 1992, only a few paved roads existed to remind us that a mining town once stood there.

It was in Claghorn that on 1 December 1992, a hunter reported seeing a seven- to eight-feet tall, apelike creature. It was dawn on the cold second day of buck season, and the witness had just walked into a wooded area when he noticed an odor resembling an "open sewer." He looked up and saw a figure covered with brownish-black hair running away from him at a distance of about 50 yards. He shot at it and then chased the creature over a hillside, where it disappeared. As usual, I did not receive this report until the following spring.

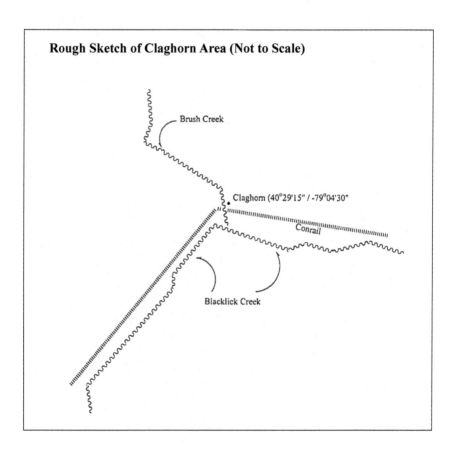

Rough Sketch of Claghorn Area (Not to Scale)

Brush Creek

Claghorn (40°29'15" / -79°04'30"

Conrail

Blacklick Creek

On Thursday, 27 May 1993, I grabbed my camcorder and headed for Claghorn. The area was no longer easily accessible by auto. I had to park some distance away and walk into the ghost town. I looked for prints and videotaped the area but saw nothing unusual.

I returned one more time with Bob Colt and Sam Sherry. We parked on Route 259 and accessed Claghorn by walking down the railroad tracks. It was a cool, cloudy day, and we walked through the area looking for tracks. At 4 PM, it started raining, so we returned home.

CHAPTER 4

Squirrels and Bigfoot Love the Chestnut

At this point, you might think that Westmoreland County Bigfoot sightings occur only in the various communities along the western base of the Chestnut Ridge. However, over the years, a number of unusual reports were obtained from hunters, campers and workers on the ridge itself.

The following account concerns the Bigfoot encounters of a Westmoreland County man named Bob France. I was aware of his sightings for several years before I finally decided to contact him. He didn't have a telephone, and no one was able to tell me precisely where he lived. After several inquiries, I located his home in Bethel Township, not far from Vandergrift, Pennsylvania. Just before dark, on the evening of 21 February 1990, I drove through an open gate and along the narrow dirt drive leading to the one-story stone house built several years earlier by Bob France. As I approached, I saw him standing in front of his home talking to a friend with whom he often went camping. Wary at first, he warmed up as he sensed my intense interest in Bigfoot. Within an hour, we were sitting at his long, oak dining room table poring through photographs and topographical maps.

In 1990, Robert Dale France was a 47-year-old man who prided himself on his abilities as an outdoorsman. He has been hiking and camping on the Chestnut Ridge since 1963. On many of his expeditions, he observed bobcats, cougars and other species rare to the Keystone State. However, the last thing in the world he expected to see was the Pennsylvania Bigfoot.

His first encounter occurred on 18 June 1982. It was near dusk as he strolled the woods of the Chestnut Ridge near Bear Cave. As he walked, Bob noticed a strange odor penetrating the area. He likened the odor to a "mixture of rotten eggs, spoiled potatoes and urine." He was heading into the valley near an old foundation to look for bottles. Just ahead, off to the side of the trail, was a large rock, and behind it stood a huge figure that prompted the witness to come to a stop. Bob observed a tall, hairy creature with its large hands on the boulder. It just stood there looking at him. The creature then stepped out from behind the rock and walked toward the startled witness. After coming within 10 feet of where Bob stood, the creature abruptly veered left and disappeared into a thicket of high weeds.

According to Bob, the creature was completely bipedal and covered with dark brown and black hair about six to eight inches in length. The head was completely covered with hair, but it did appear to have a high, broad forehead. It was too dark in the woods to distinguish facial features. The arms hung down to the knees, and each hand appeared to have five fingers. The creature was broad and husky, with shoulders slowly rising to the head, giving it the appearance of having no neck. Bob France thought the creature had an unusual gait. It had a long stride in which the entire body dipped and rose as it swung its arms with each step. Bob described it as "having an unusual hitch to its stride."

After the sighting, Bob returned to his camp along a stream about one-half mile from the cave. Two friends who had originally accompanied him to the top of the ridge had built a glowing fire. He told the couple about the encounter, ate dinner, and retired to the tent he pitched on the embankment above the run. Later that evening, coming from the stream bed, he heard heavy breathing from a chest "that seemed to rattle as it breathed, as if it had pneumonia." Then he heard something climb the five-foot embankment in one step before hitting his front tent support. It then walked into the clearing between his tent and the fire. He saw the silhouette of the tall, hairy biped as it stood there briefly before slowly walking away. His friends were sleeping on the other side of the clearing and heard nothing.

Bob enjoyed camping along Trout Run on the ridge. It was not unusual for him to carry his tent and other provisions into the area and remain there for two weeks. On one occasion in May 1989, he found several five-toed tracks along Trout Run. As we talked and drank coffee at his oak table, Bob pulled out a suitcase and showed me a plaster cast of the print of the left foot. It was 13 inches long and six inches wide at mid-foot. Except for the absence of an arch and the extreme width, it was very humanlooking. In fact, two of the toes appeared to have calluses. Before this, I had experienced only three- and four-toed footprints that did not resemble those of a hominid. It was now apparent to me that if the Pennsylvania Bigfoot was indeed a real animal, there was more than one species.

Over subsequent years, Bob discovered other evidence for the existence of Bigfoot. Another of his favorite places to visit is an area called the "Black Swamp," near the very top of the ridge. This is a one-acre, marshy area covered mainly with skunk cabbage. He has found several footprints, including a five-toed print almost identical to the one he cast at Trout Run.

Beginning in the summer of 1991, Sam Sherry started his Chestnut Ridge Bigfoot Center and began looking for the creature on a daily basis. He was retired and lived only three miles from the eastern base of the ridge. At 10 AM on 13 August 1991, Sam was in an area of large rocks just below the fire tower when he thought he might have glimpsed the creature walking down the mountain, using the large rock formation to obscure itself. He returned daily to the area, hanging food in buckets seven feet from the ground in a muddy area. The food disappeared overnight, but no footprints were nearby, and there was no other evidence that a large animal had been in the area.

Sam Sherry carrying "Bigfoot bait" on Chestnut Ridge.

Just below the rocks was a radio tower. For several months in 1992, workers had been bulldozing in the area. Sam was concerned that this activity kept the creature away, so one day he asked one of the workers when their project would be complete. Then he asked the workers whether they observed any strange animals in the area. He was told that several days earlier, 13 October, a mechanic who was repairing one of the bulldozers saw a hairy biped rushing through the forest.

Sam examined the area and found trampled ground and a large number of broken tree branches. He also learned that the day prior to this sighting, one of the bulldozer operators was driving near the fire tower when he saw a hairy, apelike creature cross the road. It was from seven to eight feet tall, with reddish-brown hair. The driver saw the figure for only a second or two. Sam measured the distance as 150 yards.

Two main roads connect the Ligonier side of the Chestnut Ridge with the town of Derry. One of the roads is four miles long, is rather desolate and runs from Austraw Road in rural Ligonier Township to Derry. We used to call it the Derry Ridge Road, but the name has been changed to Twin Maples Road.

On 29 June 1994, at 8 PM, a couple was driving west on this road toward Derry. As they approached the top of the ridge, a summer storm moved into the area, and large pellets of hail began to fall. Suddenly, a tall, hairy biped walked from the woods on their right (north) and crossed in front of their vehicle. The creature paid no attention to them and entered an old logging road on the left. It was gone in a matter of seconds. The witnesses recall only that it was very tall and completely covered with long brown hair. The logging road ultimately leads to an area called Dark Hollow.

Without stopping, the witnesses drove home and told their neighbors about the sighting. One of the neighbors investigated the logging road the next day (Thursday) and claimed to have found large footprints about 19 inches long. Sam Sherry, Director of the Chestnut Ridge Bigfoot Center, was not notified until Saturday. He immediately investigated the site, but subsequent rains had washed away all physical traces.

Interestingly, the creature was walking from an area where Sam had spent several years looking for tracks and into a region he had yet to explore. He surmised that perhaps it was caught in the storm and was heading home where there might be shelter. For the next several months, he explored Dark Hollow. As time permitted, I joined him; however, we never found any traces of the mysterious creature.

Since Sam lived on the eastern base of the Chestnut Ridge, checking daily for signs of Bigfoot was convenient. His intent was to

Sam Sherry and his Bigfoot trap.

capture one. In 1996, he designed a special snare he felt was viable for trapping the creature. Ultimately, he was able to find someone to machine it for him. For the next 10 years, Sam Sherry set his trap where he thought Bigfoot frequented. He would carry bait to various locales, loosen and moisten the ground for better detection of footprints, and set his snare. Although the bait usually disappeared, Sam was unsuccessful in trapping the elusive Sasquatch.

CHAPTER 5

East Is East and West Is West

Due to the increase in creature reports in the 1990s, PCUFOR instituted a UFO-Bigfoot hotline. The 800 number answered at the home of Joan Jeffers in Bradford, Pennsylvania. I notified all the Pennsylvania State Police barracks as well as some local law enforcement agencies of the number. Joan and I realized the limitations of such an endeavor. The number of reports that were hoaxes increased tenfold. We did receive a few interesting creature sightings that were subsequently investigated; however, on average, the sightings were two years old, which made the gathering of physical trace evidence impossible. The hotline number did increase the number of reports we received from other areas of the Keystone State.

Over the years, the Pennsylvania Bigfoot has been observed on many occasions outside of Westmoreland County. Prominent places include Indiana, Armstrong, Somerset, Fayette and Cambria counties in the western part of the state.

On 9 November 1989, I received a phone call from a Pittsburgh resident who related an encounter he and three other men had in October as they were driving in Indiana County. They were riding in a car on Route 56 several miles west of Homer City on the afternoon of 7 October 1989 when they observed a hairy, erect-walking biped step from the right side about 35 yards away. The creature crossed the road in front of them in two strides.

According to the man in the back seat behind the passenger, the creature was at least eight feet tall and completely covered with dark brown hair. Its head was round and completely hair-covered. Observed only in profile, the figure appeared slim in stature and "a bit bent over" as it walked in sort of a stiff-armed, stifflegged manner. The driver parked the car. The men climbed out and ran to where the creature disappeared. They never saw it again. On the right side of the road is Cherry Creek; on the left is a steep, unpaved road that leads to an abandoned waterworks. The witnesses assumed that before they arrived on the scene, the creature passed through the open gate, quickly walked up the road and veered left into a pine forest.

When I interviewed the driver of the vehicle, he told me the creature was closer to seven feet in height. It was a "deep brown-black in color, with different shadings at various places on the body." The hair was "sleek, not shaggy." Its head blended into the shoulders, giving the appearance of no neck. The arms were long, but not below the knees. He thought the creature was at least 100 yards away, not 35 yards, as the passenger estimated.

This case exposes the limitations of investigating the Pennsylvania Bigfoot. Our Center did not receive this report until a month after the sighting. I visited the area on 15 November and spent several hours walking through the wetlands west of Route 56, and the old abandoned waterworks high on the hill east of the highway but found no evidence. Note also the differences in the testimonies of the witnesses with respect to height and distance. The discrepancies show how unreliable witnesses' observations can be, which in turn affects our ability to uncover the source of this enigmatic creature.

Route 56 near Homer City Where A Creature Sighting Occured on 7 October 1989 (Not to Scale)

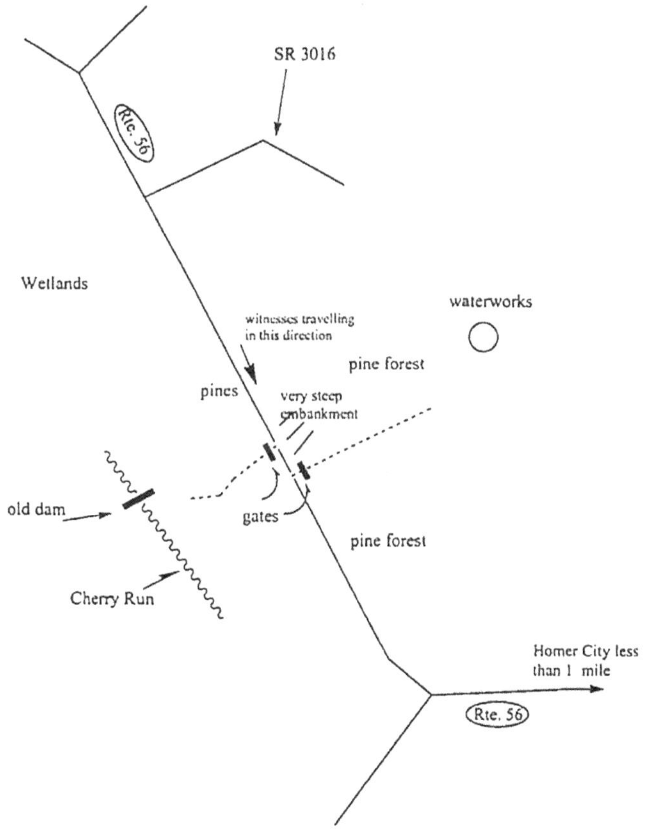

SR 3016

Rte. 56

Wetlands

witnesses travelling
in this direction

waterworks

pine forest

pines

very steep
embankment

old dam

gates

pine forest

Cherry Run

Homer City less
than 1 mile

Rte. 56

In 1992, Bigfoot appeared to move to the Laurel Mountain area. Sam Sherry received a call from a reporter for *The Ligonier Echo* wanting information on creature sightings from the village of Scullton in Somerset County. Neither he nor I was aware of the reports, so on 19 September 1992, we drove up the mountain to Scullton hoping to track down some of the witnesses. Around noon we pulled into a general store. The proprietress provided us with the names and locations of several witnesses but informed us that the sightings occurred the previous spring. She told us about an encounter in early 1992. Two boys were riding their dirt bikes near Scullton when a tall, hairy creature walked out of the woods in front of them. It was over seven feet tall and completely covered with a mixture of gray and black hair.

We then visited the home of a potential witness on Kanaul Road. He was out of town, but his daughter was home. In May 1992, her father was awakened at 3 AM when his dogs started barking frantically. He turned on the light in his back yard and saw nothing. But on his way back to bed, he looked out his living room picture window and observed a nine-foot tall creature with black, shaggy hair and long arms standing in the front yard. The man turned away to switch on the front porch light, but by the time he looked out the window again, the mysterious figure had disappeared.

While in Somerset County, I placed advertisements containing our hotline number in several of the local pennysavers, hoping the creature was still in the neighborhood. My ads resulted in one more report, but again we received it several months after the incident. On Sunday, 29 November 1992, two friends were walking in the woods on Laurel Mountain in Somerset County when they saw ill-defined tracks with long strides in the dusting of snow. After following the tracks for about three-quarters of a mile, they heard a high-pitched scream. One of the men stopped by a large tree. A few seconds later, a nine-foot tall, hairy figure brushed by him. The witness became disoriented and fell to the ground. His friend had to help him out of the woods.

This was the last creature report we received from the Laurel Mountain for many years.

In the summer of 1995, PCUFOR received several interesting UFO reports near the villages of Colver and Revloc in Cambria County. Revloc lies on Route 422, just west of Ebensburg. In 1993, a 102-megawatt cogeneration power plant was constructed in Colver. The plant uses coal refuse from a closed coal mine as fuel. Colver was founded by B. Dotson Coleman and J.H. Weaver, who developed the first mine shaft there in 1911. The name of the village is derived from the first three letters of one founder's name and the last three of the other. Revloc emerged when the Monroe Coal Company began shipping coal from there in March 1918. Revloc sits on U.S. Route 422 and is "Colver" spelled backwards.

On 29 August 1995, I received a call from a Johnstown man who reported a creature sighting near Revloc. Joe Nemanich and a friend were in a pickup truck driving west on Route 422 at 3:15 AM. Just after passing through the village of Revloc, the high beams of their headlights illuminated what they first thought was a deer crossing the road. After a second or so, the witnesses realized the creature was bipedal and completely covered with dark brown hair. The figure moved from their right to their left and was about in the middle of the two-lane highway when they first saw it. It walked into the woods and disappeared. The excited witnesses stopped, turned the vehicle around, and shined the headlights into the woods, but were unable to see it again. When first observed, the creature was about 100 yards away, so they were unable to observe any facial details. Joe noticed the figure was very broad at the shoulders and narrow at the waist. Although the night was clear, he also thought the legs were "fuzzy," as if shrouded in a mist. The other witness did not notice this.

On September 3, Sam Sherry and I accompanied Joe Nemanich to Revloc, where he recreated his Bigfoot encounter. North of Route 422 is a large reservoir, and south of the highway is a power substation. The creature could have quickly vacated the area by walking along the power line right-of-way. We found no physical traces during our September visit to the locale. Later that year, several people were traveling by car west on 422 when they observed a large, circular multi-colored object descend toward a ballfield at Revloc. Within a few seconds it ascended vertically and disappeared at a terrific speed. Then on 2 November, at 5

AM, several Colver residents called 911 to report strange flashes of light over the town. When the police investigated, the sky was clear, and they were unable to find the source of the light.

When I began investigating Bigfoot in Pennsylvania, I assumed the creature was indigenous to the western part of the state. It wasn't until the early 1980s that reports began to pop up in eastern Pennsylvania. On the afternoon of 18 July 1980, a man in Columbia County watched a tall, hairy biped walk down a railroad bed toward him. He stated that the creature was between seven and eight feet tall, weighed 400 pounds, and had long, black hair over most of its body. It had a large head, a flattened nose, large eyes, and arms that swung well below its knees. The creature suddenly turned and ran into the bushes, at which time a frightened deer ran across the tracks. In 1985, the creature was sighted in Annville, Pennsylvania, not far from Harrisburg, the state capital. Reports began again in the early 1990s. Although separated in distance, the sightings were generally in the Williamsport area.

Around dawn on 7 June 1991, two men stood beside their vehicle on White Deer Creek Road in Union County, Pennsylvania. This was a forestry road in a highly wooded region of the township. Suddenly the two heard loud noises in the woods. A creek runs through the area, but it is at a lower level than the road. The men looked up and saw a deer run up the embankment from the creek and cross the road about 40 feet ahead of them. However, the noises continued, and then they saw a "tall jogger" trot diagonally up the embankment to the road. They quickly realized the figure was not human. It was a tall, hairy creature walking perfectly erect on two legs.

The astonished witnesses heard the creature's heavy breathing as it stopped at the edge of the forestry road about 30 feet away. They estimated that it weighed about 450 pounds. The creature put its hands on its hips "as if it were about to strike a pose," but instead, it ran one hand over its hips to the thighs. Its arm hung about two inches above the knee. The creature appeared to have a human-like, five-fingered hand. It was between seven and eight feet tall, and was completely covered with long, stringy brown hair, the color of muddy creek water. A patch on the belly appeared darker in color. The hair on the face was not as thick and long as that on the head, which enabled the witnesses to see the eyes. They were large and black with no white part or glow to them. The nose did not protrude to a large degree, and ears were not discernable.

At first, the men detected no odor, but within a few seconds, a "sour, sweaty" smell permeated the air. The animal was breathing hard and stopped to look at the witnesses, who in turn stared back in awe. The figure stood there and glared at them. It seemed to move its thin lips as if it wanted to say something, but it never opened its mouth to show any teeth.

After about a minute, the creature took a step toward the men, so they hastily climbed into their vehicle. As they peered through the windshield, they saw the creature turn and walk in the opposite direction. Then it broke into a trot and disappeared into the woods. The witnesses later examined the area for footprints. The ground was too dry for indentations; however, in a dusty area, the men claimed to have seen a 16-inch, five-toed imprint.

Not far away in Clinton County, another incident occurred several weeks later, in June 1991. A young man and his friend were fishing at Long Run in LeMar Township around one o'clock in the afternoon. The terrain along the bank was hilly and wooded, and the nearest residence was a cabin about one-half mile away. The men suddenly heard footfalls, like someone running, but the sounds "were very loud, like a boulder rolling down a mountain." When they looked toward the sound, the witnesses observed a seven-foot tall, hairy creature running on two legs. They watched it for several seconds before it disappeared behind bushes about 30 feet away. They immediately vacated the area. The witnesses said the strange entity had long, dark brown hair. It ran erect like a man and weighed about 400 pounds. The only facial features observed were the eyes, which were completely black, and the forehead, which was flat.

Later that summer, I advertised our hotline number in various newspapers in the Williamsport area. As a result, a few other sightings from eastern Pennsylvania surfaced. In March 1990, four men were camping on Cedar Run, north of Lock Haven. They were in their tents around 11 PM when they heard a "drawn out, loud, screeching yell."

Stunned and scared, two of the men crawled from their tents and began building up the campfire. Looking around, they were unable to see anything, so they shined flashlights into the woods. They saw two sets of yellow eyes about the size of pineapple rings. They even noticed that the eyes blinked. One pair of eyes was about seven feet from the ground; the other, 10 feet. They appeared to be the eyes of shadowy, bipedal creatures that stood on the ground. As the men walked toward the eyes, the figures turned and ran up the hill. As the witnesses returned to the campsite, they saw another set of the yellow eyes near their tent. Waving and yelling, the men ran toward the tent, scaring the creature off. The next day, they examined the area for tracks, but found nothing unusual.

A rare sighting of a family of creatures occurred near Cedar Run in May 1991. An elderly couple was driving on a back road around 10 PM, near Renovo, Pennsylvania, when they saw illuminated in their headlight beams three hairy creatures cross the road. They appeared to be a male, a female and a juvenile. All three were completely covered with dark hair and walked erect on two legs. The creatures paid no attention to the vehicle. They simply continued walking, stepped over a guardrail and disappeared into the woods.

One of the more interesting Clinton County sightings occurred in the middle of the afternoon on 22 June 1990. A man was driving his pickup truck on Old Schoolhouse Road in Bald Eagle Township when he turned into Lusk Road and saw movement from the corner of his eye. It turned out to be a tall, hairy creature hopping over the guardrail on the right side of the road. It put one hand on the rail and jumped over with two feet.

The witness slammed on the brakes and stopped within 10 feet of the animal. The car behind him, containing a man, a woman and two children, also stopped. The witness removed his sunglasses and observed the creature standing there looking over the vehicles and the occupants. He described the creature as tall, between seven and eight feet, and grotesque, with long, shaggy, matted hair. The hair was tangled, knotted and chocolate-brown in color. The face was hair-covered, and the pickup truck driver noticed only its eyes, which moved as it slowly surveyed the witnesses. The eyes were very dark in the center and lighter around the outside. They were almond-shaped and about the size of a quarter. He noticed no other facial features. The head was round and sat on a very short, thick neck. In fact, the creature appeared to have almost no neck. It had a muscular build, and its arms were very long. The fingered hands dangled about four feet from the ground.

The creature suddenly started walking toward the pickup truck at a diagonal, heading for the opposite side of the road. It was then that the driver noticed a terrible odor emanating from the creature. "It was like the stench of old, rotting garbage," he said. When the figure reached the opposite shoulder of the road, it hesitated a second to look again at the vehicles. Then, emitting a pig-like grunt, it walked down a slight bank and disappeared into the woods.

In his rearview mirror, the pickup truck driver saw the man in the car behind his start to leave his vehicle. Then, as though he thought better of it, he disappeared back inside and closed the door. Both men drove away without exchanging comments. The witness returned the following day to look for prints but found none. The ground was dry and hard. He did notice that the creature entered the highway by following a well-worn path from a pond below the right side of the road.

As these sightings were occurring in eastern Pennsylvania throughout 1990-1991, Sam Sherry continued his efforts to locate Bigfoot again in the western part of the state. Nearly every day he drove from Wilpen to the fire tower at the top of the Chestnut Ridge, parked his Jeep and spent the day walking the woods. If Sam found an area where he saw possible tracks, he would conceal himself for hours, hoping to see the creature again and capture it on film. Just before heading home, he would leave food in an area where an animal would have to leave tracks while eating. All his attempts were unsuccessful. On weekends, I would join him as we roamed the ridge from dawn to dusk, but to no avail.

Sam wrote letters to *The Ligonier Echo*, a local weekly newspaper, describing his attempts to locate Bigfoot. Occasionally, the letter would be printed, resulting in a few old creature reports. One of these was from a farmer on the Ligonier side of the ridge above Darlington. Sometime during the spring of 1990, he heard high-pitched screams originating behind his home. He shined a flashlight through a window and observed a hairy, apelike creature standing in his pasture. The figure was about five feet tall and had "red glowing eyes." The farmer's horses were spooked and ran to the other end of the fenced pasture.

Sam and I visited the farm in January 1991. We found a long power line right-of-way next to the farm, which would permit any animal easy access to the pasture. There are a series of caves near the area; however, our examination of these did not produce any unusual tracks in the snow.

CHAPTER 6

Those Funny Big Tracks in the Snow

As 1992 ended and I began doing my statistics, I realized that 1991 and 1992 provided more legitimate creature reports than any previous two-year period. I was optimistic that 1993 would do the same. In January, I received a call from a teenage boy in Washington County who was eager to tell me about a series of strange occurrences in and around his home. Although the incidents involved a Bigfoot-like creature, the majority of the encounters occurred in 1991 and 1992. It appeared that, as usual, I received the reports too late for an in-depth investigation.

On 18 January 1993, I drove to Washington County to interview the teenager, his brother and his mother. Their home was an old, two-story brick farmhouse on West McMurray Road near Morganza, about one mile east of Canonsburg, the hometown of Perry Como and Bobby Vinton. As usual, I arrived in the area early, drove around and took pictures before I knocked on the witnesses' door.

Probably one of the most enigmatic aspects of Bigfoot sightings is that they do not always occur in isolated, rural areas. In fact, it is not unusual for a creature to be sighted in the backyard of a house that sits along a road close to other homes. The region is not quite suburban, but then, it isn't rural either. I started referring to these localities as "rurburbia." It was quite apparent that this was one of those areas.

Upon meeting the family, I was led to their living room, where I sat amongst several cats and dogs while I conducted the interview. Strange things occurred in their backyard in the fall of 1991 and again in the summer of 1992. After dark on the evening of 21 September 1991 the teenager observed an eight-foot tall, hairy bipedal creature behind his home. It was only 30 yards away; however, he noticed it made no noise as it walked with its arms swinging back and forth below the knees. It was exceptionally thin and covered with black hair. It simply "faded from view" for no apparent reason.

The following summer, the two brothers heard strange noises in the backyard. A relative became interested in the occurrences. Her name was Judy, and she began spending every weekend after dark behind the farmhouse waiting for things to happen. One dark evening in July, they saw five hairy, bipedal creatures with green eyes standing in a neighbor's yard. One was at least 12 feet tall, but the others were much shorter. Another eight-foot tall, green-eyed creature was observed later that summer. At the rear of their yard is a garden. Behind the garden, a steep embankment leads to railroad tracks that parallel West McMurray Road. One evening at dusk, the two brothers and a friend were walking east along the tracks. At a distance they saw a tall, hairy figure standing at the train trestle over Chartiers Creek. When the creature saw the boys, it apparently crawled down the embankment toward the creek.

After interviewing the witnesses, I surveyed the area behind their home. The embankment to the railroad tracks was too steep, so the boys had attached a strong rope to a tree so we could easily climb up and down the hillside.

More snow fell in February and March 1993 than in any of the previous 20 years. On Saturday, 13 March 1993, a blizzard moved up the east coast and buried western Pennsylvania in over two feet of snow. I spent many weekends walking the railroad tracks that paralleled West McMurray Road; however, I didn't find any unusual tracks in the snow. What I did not know was that this would change the following winter.

I didn't realize it at the time, but our hotline number was to receive only a few calls in 1993. This gave me more free time, so I spent many evenings that summer of 1993 sitting in the backyard with Judy and the teenage boy who originally called me. From about 10 PM to 2 AM, we sat on benches near their garden or walked the tracks back and forth to the trestle over the Chartiers Creek. Except for an occasional strange noise or heavy footfalls in the brush, nothing unusual was observed.

However, other reports from Washington County, some old, some recent, were received by our Center. In one such case, a young woman was driving around 10 PM near Wylandville during the summer 1992 when a creature walked down a steep slope and crossed the road in front of her car. It was apelike, between seven and eight feet tall, and covered with dark, shaggy hair. Suddenly another tall biped, followed by two shorter ones, crossed the road. Frightened, the witness quickly drove away.

More snow and ice arrived in late 1993 into the winter of 1994. To my surprise, it was during this inclement weather that Bigfoot returned. Most of the early reports were of tracks found in the snow in Washington County, especially around California, a small college town that sits on the Monongahela River. Flowing in a northerly direction, the river literally snakes its way through coal towns such as Newell, Elco, Roscoe, Charleroi, Monessen and Donora, before emptying into the Ohio River at Pittsburgh. The snow began on January 4, dumping nearly 15 inches in the area. Rain, ice and more snow followed the next week before temperatures plummeted to minus 15 degrees Fahrenheit over the weekend of the 15th, and minus 25 degrees F. on January 19. Another ice storm on the 27th was followed by more snow. Then on February 1 came the report of large tracks.

A caretaker at the Mount Zion Church in the Crescent Heights section of West Pike Run Township was burning trash behind the building when he saw a set of large tracks in the snow. The footprints were 31 inches long, 17 inches wide and with four toes. The witness stated that the tracks were so clear one could see snow coming up between the toes.

An investigator from Coal Center visited the area the next day and found there were two sets of prints, a 31-inch track and a 17-inch one. The tracks were depressed several inches into the snow, even though it was hard-crusted due to the ice storm. In fact, the 215-pound investigator made no indentations in the snow as he walked through the area. The smaller creature appeared to be lame, judging by an imperfection in its right foot. A story about the footprint finds appeared in the 4 February 1994 issue of *The Pittsburgh Press*. As a result of the publicity, dozens of residents wandered over the church ground, destroying the evidence before I was able to see it.

Although no creature was observed in this case, the incident prompted a Crescent Heights couple to report a sighting that occurred five years earlier. They witnessed a nine-foot tall, bipedal figure in their backyard, at a distance of about 100 feet. It had long, reddish-brown hair and green eyes. The creature streaked into the woods, slapping the trees with its arms as it ran. It remained in the woods for a period of time, emitting loud, high-pitched screams. The same family had also recently seen large tracks in the snow.

Then late Saturday evening, 5 February 1994, I received a call from the West McMurray Road residents. One of their neighbors saw a hairy creature earlier that afternoon. I drove to Canonsburg the following morning to interview the witness. This particular area is called Van Emman. The woman's home sits on a hill, and the kitchen window in the rear of the house overlooks a stream and a large field about 150 yards away. From the window, she observed a tall figure walking through the field. It was much taller than a human, completely covered with black hair, and walking with tremendously long strides. The head was hair-covered, and the creature appeared to have no neck. The woman quickly called her son to the window, but he observed only the long, hairy legs as it walked into the woods at the edge of Chartiers Creek. Most of the field was covered with snow that had fallen several

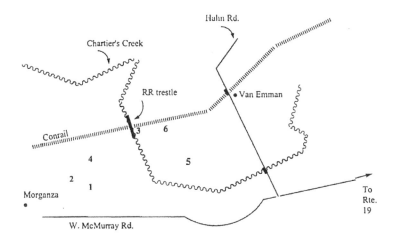

Morganza-Van Emman Sighting Area

1. Creature sighted on 21 September 1991
2. Five creatures observed in a backyard during July 1992
3. Creature observed at RR trestle in the summer 1992
4. Creature observed standing near a tree in Aug. or Sept. 1992
5. Creature observed walking through a field on 5 Feb. 1994
6. Large 5-toed footprints found in the snow on Feb. 1994

days earlier; however, there were large patches of barren ground. Upon investigation of the entire field, I found no prints in the snow. I suspected a hoax, even though the neighbors vouched for the witness' veracity. It would be impossible for the creature she described to cross the field without leaving imprints. This was just another example of the unusual properties of the Pennsylvania Bigfoot.

It was still early and the skies were clear, so several of us decided to broaden the search area. On the hill above the other side of the field were the railroad tracks that ran behind the home of the original creature witnesses that brought me to this area a year earlier. Along these tracks, we found a series of large imprints in the snow. They were five-toed, 18 inches long, and 8.5 inches wide at mid-foot. The step distance from the heel of the right foot to the heel of the left foot was 50 inches. I am six feet, six inches tall, and my walking step distance in the snow was only 22 inches. The imprints continued for about 150 yards before veering to the right, over the hillside and into the field where we previously found no tracks. The longitudinal arch at mid-foot, due to walking motion, was clearly present. This was not a "cookie cutter" fake. The imprints were about two inches deep and appeared to be from 24 to 48 hours old. Melt-out was minimal, since all the tracks were the same size, and the toe imprints were not yet obscured.

Where the tracks came from is still a mystery. They began at the railroad trestle on the east side of Chartiers Creek. We were unable to find any prints on the west side, although the area was completely covered with snow. We found no tracks along the creek below the bridge; however, some of this area was not snow covered. Interestingly, this is the same trestle where the three boys observed Bigfoot during summer of 1992.

Two days later, on February 8, large footprints were reported in suburban Washington, Pennsylvania. Three teenagers were playing in the woods above their house when they found a number of footprints in the snow. An ice storm later that evening destroyed the prints, but the boys claimed that whatever made them appeared to be bipedal.

Bigfoot snow prints.

Whenever possible during the last three weeks of February, I hiked through the woods in and around Crescent Heights, Daisytown and Van Emman. Despite my efforts, I found no unusual tracks.

Other examples of Bigfoot in "rurburbia" occurred on and around South Montour Road, only 20 miles north of downtown Pittsburgh. They happened throughout most of 1975 and were explored by Joan Jeffers and other investigators from the Pennsylvania Center for UFO Research.

It was after dark on 29 December 1974 when two young boys looked out the family living room window to see the evergreen tree their father had beautifully decorated with multi-colored lights. The boys were quite surprised when they observed a huge hair-covered but man-like beast standing at the base of the tree as if mesmerized by the brilliant lights. The excited youths yelled for their parents who came to the window in time to see the back of the creature as it ran into the woods at the edge of the property line. The parents surmised that the screams of their sons had compelled the animal to retreat hastily.

The next morning, Joan Jeffers found large, well-defined footprints in the muddy ground. The tracks were 16 inches long with four toes. Measuring 12 inches wide at the toes, and six inches wide at the heel, they were definitely not just a large human print. The running stride of the creature was an incredible 14 feet, and the investigators were able to follow the tracks until they were lost on the rocky ground at the edge of the woods.

Five months later, in the same area near North Park, two schoolteachers were driving along Harts Run Road around 1AM. The meeting they had attended lasted an exceptionally long time, and both women were eager to get home. After the driver negotiated a curve in the highway, her passenger suddenly shouted, "Look out! There's a man in the road!" The teacher slammed on the brakes, and both observed a 12-foot tall figure with glowing red eyes. It was bipedal and completely covered with hair. It easily walked up a steep embankment and disappeared into the woods.

Joan Jeffers investigated two days later and found 21-inch, three-toed tracks. The tracks were five feet apart on the 45-degree embankment. Joan followed the prints another 700 feet along the damp forest floor before they suddenly disappeared. This was quite surprising since the basic soil texture had not changed, and there was still a distance of 300 feet before reaching the edge of a wooded area with hard, rocky ground. The tracks simply vanished!

In March 1975, two women in an automobile turned into South Montour Road after dark and headed north. It is now paved; however, 30 years ago it was a narrow, rutted dirt road. Within a few minutes, they saw a seven-foot tall, apelike creature with orange eyes walking along the left side of the road. According to the young ladies, it turned abruptly and walked "into," "not up," the hillside and vanished.

In February 2006 I noticed a creature report on a website. It occurred in an area not far from South Montour Road. The witnesses' names were not given, so I was unable to investigate the report. However, I decided to visit the locale and look around when I had some free time.

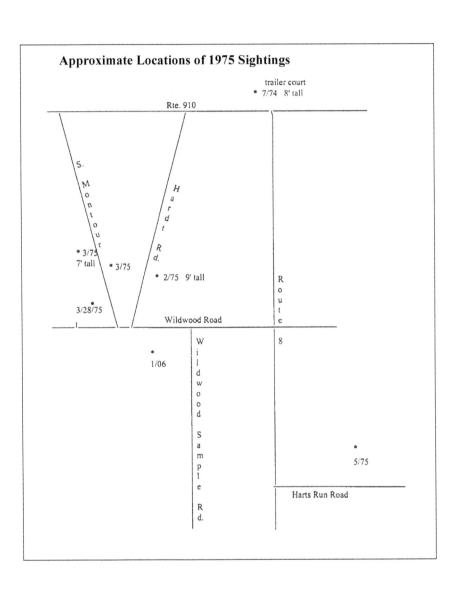

Approximate Locations of 1975 Sightings

trailer court
* 7/74   8' tall

Rte. 910

S. Montour

Hardt Rd.

* 3/75
7' tall
* 3/75

* 2/75   9' tall

Route 8

*
3/28/75

Wildwood Road

*
1/06

Wildwood Sample Rd.

*
5/75

Harts Run Road

The afternoon of 6 March 2006 was a bright, sunny day, so after work I drove the 20 miles to north Pittsburgh. Around 3 PM I was standing along Wildwood Road near the flea market looking towards Wildwood-Sample Road with binoculars. An SUV passed by and slowed as it crossed the bridge. I thought it might be the police wondering what I was doing. The SUV turned around, came back across the bridge and parked next to my Jeep. A man in a three-piece suit climbed out and inquired what I was doing. I told him I headed an organization that studied the appearance of strange animals that didn't seem to belong in certain areas. I did not mention Bigfoot or the fact that I was investigating bipedal creatures. He replied that he stopped because he was hoping I had seen what he had observed in January, and he wanted me to tell him he wasn't crazy.

According to the witness it was late afternoon, and he was heading toward Route 8. As he was crossing the bridge, he looked at the hillside to his right and saw a tall, dark, hairy figure walking up the hill toward the woods. It was walking on two legs, taking tremendous strides. It appeared to be several times larger than the average man. He was able to observe it only for a few seconds before he had to look back in the direction he was driving. Shocked, he turned around and returned, but the creature was no longer there. He assumed it disappeared into the woods at the top of the hill.

From 1978-1984, Bell Township, near the town of Apollo in Westmoreland County, produced a series of Bigfoot reports. Many of the sightings centered around a family living in an old farmhouse along Route 819. The main witnesses were Sam Frew, his wife Ruth and their 12-year-old son. Their two-story farmhouse, rented from a landlord who lived in Pittsburgh, sat high on a hill above the Kiskiminetas River near the town of Apollo. Also on the property were a small cabin, an old, abandoned one-room schoolhouse and a weathered barn. The family's nearest neighbors were about 1,000 yards away. Above the Frew home was one of the highest points in Westmoreland. The point was called "round top" by the local residents.

Rough diagram of the area where the creature was sighted in January 2006 in the late afternoon. The roads and stream are not straight as drawn, and the sketch is not scale.

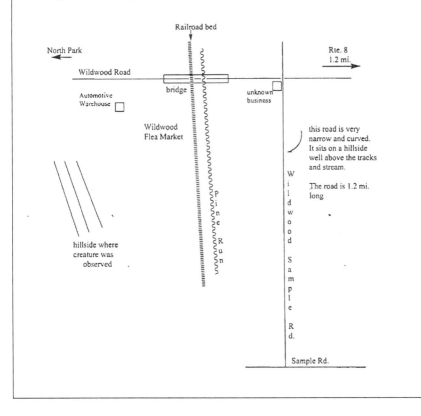

Railroad bed

North Park

Rte. 8
1.2 mi.

Wildwood Road

bridge

Automotive
Warehouse

unknown
business

Wildwood
Flea Market

this road is very
narrow and curved.
It sits on a hillside
well above the tracks
and stream.

The road is 1.2 mi.
long

Pine Run

Wildwood Sample Rd.

hillside where
creature was
observed

Sample Rd.

In 1979, the Frew family and several of their neighbors began hearing eerie growling and hissing sounds. The vocalizations were loud and usually preceded by a cessation of the normal night noises of the crickets and tree frogs. Although the incidents happened periodically over the next two years, they seemed to occur most often between April and November. However, this might simply reflect the fact that the witnesses spent more time indoors with the windows closed from December through March. Ruth Frew kept a journal of the incidents, and the family began referring to the culprit as "Mystery." Sam mapped the area, numbering the sections where the creature was heard. By the time our research center entered the case, 34 numbers appeared on his map.

On 18 April 1981, Sam Frew had the opportunity to briefly observe Mystery. At around 10 PM, the Frews were in their living room watching TV when they heard a loud, shrill call outside. Sam grabbed his rifle and flashlight before heading out the door toward the ever-familiar vocalization. Sam followed the sound up the hill to the field behind his house. He turned and walked along a path that paralleled the field. To his right in the flashlight beam, he saw a figure walking in the woods. It was bipedal, very wide and heavy, but only about four feet tall. It was completely covered with hair and had large, reddish-orange eyes. While holding both the rifle barrel and the flashlight in his left hand, Sam shot at the creature, which at this time was about 50 yards away. He doesn't know whether he hit it, but after the shot was fired, he was unable to see the creature anymore. Rather than investigating any further, the witness retraced his steps to the farmhouse.

He returned to the area the next day but found no traces of blood. No footprints were visible in the hard soil. The Frews later called the police, who gave them our hotline number. We began our investigation on 25 April 1981. At the time, Sam did not connect Mystery to the Bigfoot phenomenon, and neither did our investigators. After all, the thing Sam observed was not very tall.

The situation changed on 12 August 1981. Sam was walking along a gas line right-of-way on the other side of Route 819 when he sensed someone was following him. Sam couldn't see anything due to the dense thickets, but he could hear movement to his right. As he reached an opening, he saw a tall figure step over the pipeline and disappear into the woods. He estimated that it was nearly 12 feet tall and had hair over most of its body. Later that month, while riding his bike on Route 819, a young boy happened to glance down into a pasture across from the Frew farm. There he observed the back of a 10-feet tall, apelike creature as it walked slowly from the pasture into the woods. He said it had brownish-black hair, a cone-shaped head and no neck.

Creature sightings continued to occur along Route 819 into 1984. From 1981-1984, I spent over 600 hours at the Frew farm, investigating these cases and trying to solve this mystery, all to no avail. In 1985, Ruth Frew died, and Sam eventually moved away.

In 2006 I received an e-mail from Eric Altman, and it was *déjà vu* all over again.

A woman named Lisa reported the sighting of a hairy man on Route 819 in Bell Township. Since I was familiar with the area, Eric asked me to investigate the case.

On 2 December 2006 Eric and I met with Lisa at a restaurant where 819 intersects Route 66. She provided us with the following information:

She was driving her SUV at a speed of about 55 mph on two-lane Route 819, heading north toward Route 66. It was mid-September 2006 around 6 PM and still daylight as she came over a rise and began heading downhill. About 0.2 miles away the witness saw what she thought was a man running down the driveway of a farm toward Route 819. Within a few seconds she observed that it was unclothed, completely covered with short reddish-brown hair and no taller than six feet.

For a split second she imagined it was a deer on two legs. It was moving from left to right across her field of view. The figure ran across Route 819 on to Bell Point Road where she lost sight of it. It never looked in her direction or paid any attention to her vehicle. The witness then

Rough Sketch (not to scale) of the Bell Point Area of Westmoreland County

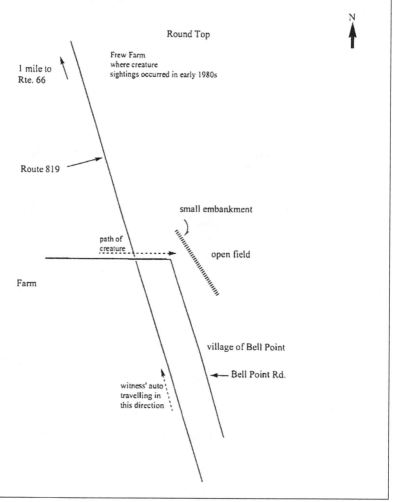

N

Round Top

Frew Farm
where creature
sightings occurred in early 1980s

1 mile to
Rte. 66

Route 819

small embankment

path of
creature

open field

Farm

village of Bell Point

Bell Point Rd.

witness' auto
travelling in
this direction

accelerated the SUV, but when she reached the intersection and looked to her right, the creature was no longer there. She was confused because there was only a small embankment and an open field. The figure should still have been visible. The entire episode lasted less than 10 seconds.

She turned onto Bell Point Road, looked around in dismay, then continued on to Apollo. Lisa did not think the figure was apelike and made no connection to Bigfoot, so she did not immediately attempt to report it. She was unable to provide any further information about the creature except that it had very long arms. She saw no facial details and did not recall any unusual features about the head.

I came away from the interview with the impression that the witness was telling the truth. If Lisa wanted to hoax a Bigfoot sighting, she would have described a very tall, hairy, apelike creature. This was her first sighting; however, she had always lived in the area and was vaguely aware that reports were occurring in Bell Township in the early 1980s.

Around 11 AM we left the restaurant, and I followed Lisa up Route 819 to the sighting area. At the top of the hill was the Frew farm. The old house was still there, but much of the landscape had changed in the last 20 years. The old school house had been razed, and the area was now enclosed by an electric fence.

It was cold and windy as we arrived at Lisa's sighting locale. I spent about an hour in the area and took several pictures. I agreed with Lisa that it would have been impossible for the figure to have disappeared within the two or three seconds required for her to arrive at the intersection.

The preceding examples from Allegheny and Westmoreland Counties also provide evidence for another characteristic of the Pennsylvania Bigfoot: there appears to be many more than one species of the creature. In Pittsburgh's north hills, both three-toed and four-toed animals were observed. In Bell Township there were variations from a very tall apelike creature to a much shorter, hairy one not really resembling an ape. Although I never saw this type of creature, it has been reported in the past [for example, see Case 6205 in the Appendix], and in my own mind, I imagined that it resembled the Neanderthal-like actors in an insurance television commercial.

Chapter 7

A Paralysis of Analysis

How can one go about solving the Bigfoot phenomenon in Pennsylvania? The answer wasn't clear when I started my investigations in 1977, and it isn't clear today. Joan Jeffers and I thought about that question 30 years ago when we began gathering the information for our first book, which was printed in 1985. At the time, the Sasquatch was the enigma that it still is today. We decided that our only recourse was to take advantage of the data we had collected. Perhaps analysis of this information would provide us with an answer.

There is a tendency for sightings to occur in certain counties as opposed to others. In fact, it appears the creature has a preference for specific locales within the county. A number of sightings are often reported in one region over a six- to nine-month period before subsiding. Then, all of a sudden, the creature returns many years later. Why the Pennsylvania Bigfoot re-visits these areas is unknown; however, understanding the reason may tell us what this phenomenon is all about.

Joan and I began by looking for places where there was a greater likelihood of Bigfoot being reported. Table I shows the breakdown of sightings by county. Obviously, over the years our investigators spent most of their time hunting for Bigfoot in Westmoreland County, where nearly 40 percent of the encounters occurred.

Table I. Number of Creature Sightings by County 1901-2005*

County	Sightings	County	Sightings
Westmoreland	171	Bradford	4
Allegheny	34	Elk	4
Somerset	24	Greene	4
Washington	22	Jefferson	4
Fayette	19	Lycoming	4
Armstrong	18	McKean	4
Indiana	11	Beaver	3
Cambria	10	Chester	3
Lancaster	9	Luzerne	3
Columbia	8	Potter	3
Clearfield	7	Centre	2
Lebanon	6	Sullivan	2
York	6	Mifflin	2
Clinton	5	Snyder	1
Butler	5	Bedford	1
Mercer	5	Blair	1
Northumberland	5	Forest	1
Cameron	4	Carbon	1
Venango	4	Dauphin	1
Union	4	Perry	1
Lawrence	4	Fulton	1

* Sighting numbers from 1999-2005 courtesy of the Pennsylvania Bigfoot Society.

As shown in Table II, creature sightings predominate in certain specific areas for a period of time. It might be for a month or two, or even for several years, as in the case of the Bell Township creature reports.

Table II. Bigfoot Hot Spots

Time Frame	Location	County
April-September 1977	Cadogan	Armstrong
1978-1984	Bell Township	Westmoreland
November '79-November '80	Kingwood	Somerset
August-September 1985	N. Annville-Harrisburg	Lebanon
1988-1989	Gray Station-Derry	Westmoreland
Spring 1990-Summer 1991	Williamsport area	Clinton, Union, Lycoming
Fall 1991-Fall 1992	Canonsburg	Washington
Fall 1991-Spring 1992	Scullton	Somerset

CHASING THE ELUSIVE PENNSYLVANIA BIGFOOT

Are there certain days, months or seasons in which Bigfoot is likely to be present? The graph below shows it is apparent that the creature has no preference for a specific day of the week. Reports are fairly evenly distributed over all seven days with only a slight increase on Saturday and Sunday. This is not really surprising since more people are likely to be outdoors during the weekend.

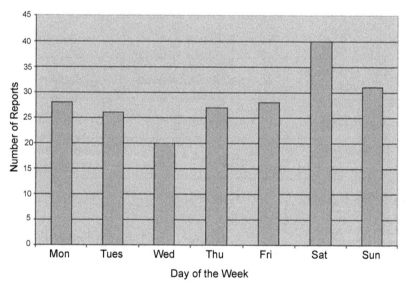

Creature Reports by Day of the Week

The graph of monthly reports indicates that sightings increase in late spring and peak in August. Again, this might be due to potential witnesses spending more time hiking, biking, and camping during the warmer months. There are sightings during the winter months. Surprisingly, the presence of a million deer and bear hunters, who are looking for animals in the woods during most of November and December, has no effect the frequency of Bigfoot reports.

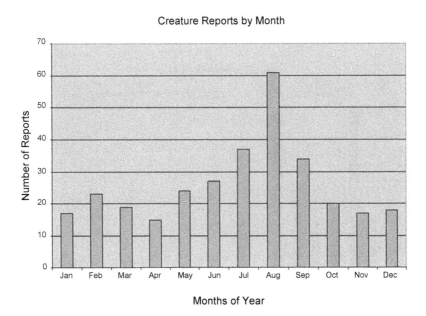

Creature Reports by Month

The Pennsylvania Bigfoot appears to prefer certain years to others. Like UFO sightings, creature reports also occur in "flaps." The number of reports from 2000-2004 was provided to me by the Pennsylvania Bigfoot Society. Notice in the next graph below that after increasing in intensity from 1991-1992, Bigfoot sightings drop nearly to zero in 1993. The creature does show a slight preference for even-numbered years. For the last 10 to 12 years, the number of reports in Pennsylvania has been quite low. This is most likely due to the internet and to the fact that most households now have computers. There are currently so many Bigfoot websites that most of our sightings are reported to hundreds of organizations not located in Pennsylvania. As a result, the creature sightings are not always investigated.

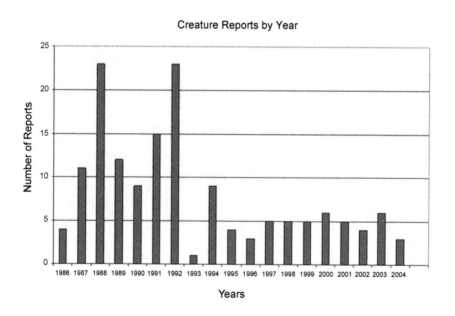

Creature Reports by Year

Using the results of these tables and graphs has never led to firsthand observations or photographs of the Pennsylvania Bigfoot. I spent thousands of hours staking out many of the hotspot locations from 1977-1997 with no success. Even concentrating on Westmoreland County near or on the Chestnut Ridge during weekends of even-numbered years was fruitless.

At the beginning of the new millennium, several more cryptozoology organizations appeared on the Pennsylvania landscape. Investigators from these organizations have continued staking out various places where creature activity predominates. In some cases, stakeouts involved a dozen or so investigators utilizing cameras and other instrumentation. As of the summer of 2017, there is still no photograph of the Pennsylvania Bigfoot.

Footprints

Another approach is to examine the physical evidence, such as footprints. The evidence definitely suggests the existence of a large bipedal creature; however, there is a problem. The footprint characteristics of the creature found in Pennsylvania are not consistent over the years. In the 1970s, many of the imprints found were not those of a primate. They were usually flat-footed with only three or four toes. It appeared as if more than one species of the Pennsylvania Bigfoot exists.

Four-toed cast 29 December 1974

There have been many other three-, four- and five-toed footprints discovered in conjunction with creature sightings over the years. Within these three categories, different foot shapes and other characteristics have been observed. It is thus apparent that if the Pennsylvania Bigfoot is indeed a hominid, a large variety of different species are present. This is also substantiated by the overall descriptions of the Pennsylvania Bigfoot provided by witnesses. These vary from creatures that are very short and Neanderthal-looking to those that are tall and apelike. Contemporary

Plaster cast of four-toed Bigfoot footprint.

anthropologists already deny that a hominid like Australopithecus robustus survived and is now responsible for Sasquatch reports. Can you imagine trying to convince these scientists that a dozen or so other species still exist today? So, our analysis was paralyzing. Next to having an actual specimen in the laboratory, or perhaps a legitimate photograph, a footprint was probably the best physical trace available. However, instead of leading us to an answer, it carried us farther away.

The imprint shown in the photo was found by Joan Jeffers when she investigated the sighting in northern Pittsburgh on 29 December 1974, as discussed earlier in the book.

Five-toed cast 23 March 1991

The next plaster cast was provided by Bob France. He found a trail of prints in the Black Swamp area of the Chestnut Ridge on 23 March 1991. The distance between steps was more than twice that of a man running at high speed. Although no creature was sighted, I am presuming this is the cast of the right foot of a Pennsylvania Sasquatch. Notice that it is quite different than the one found in 1974. The 1991 print appears to be more human-like, in that it has five toes, with a prominent large toe, and the tips of all five line up on a slight diagonal across the front.

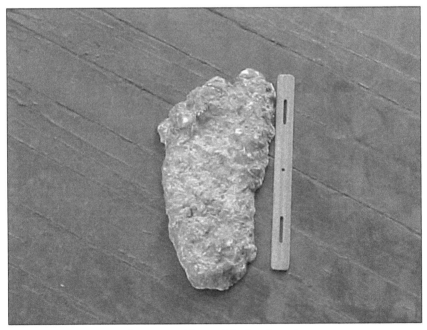

Plaster cast of five-toed Bigfoot footprint.

However, there are differences between this purported Sasquatch foot and a human one. Bigfoot appears to be flat-footed, and the four small toes are about the same size. Table III provides characteristic variations between the 1991 imprint and my human foot. The most prominent difference is the width of the creature's print. Its width is about half of the length. This is very typical of Pennsylvania Bigfoot prints found in the last 20 years, including the one found in the snow in Washington County. Note: the width of my foot is only 25 percent of the length.

Table III. Comparison of a Pennsylvania Bigfoot Print to the Author's Foot

Characteristic	Author	Pennsylvania Bigfoot
Height	6 feet, 5 inches	7 to 8 feet
Weight	185 pounds	unknown
Length of foot	12 inches	13 inches
Width at mid-foot	3 inches	6 inches
Length of big toe	2 ⅝ inches	2 ½ inches
Width of big toe	1 ¼ inches	2 inches
Length of smallest toe	1 ¼ inches	1 ½ inches

It is difficult for an anthropology novice such as myself to analyze hominid footprints. Like many other people in the Sasquatch field, I use the excellent information published by Grover S. Krantz in his book, *Big Footprints: A Scientific Inquiry into the Reality of Sasquatch* (Johnson Books, Boulder, Colorado, 1992). For example, the toes of the 1991 plaster cast are about the same size as mine, even though the foot is larger. Krantz proposes that this is ideal for a Sasquatch because short toes can be flexed with more power. This increases the creature's grasping ability when climbing steep hills or maneuvering in muddy areas. Krantz goes on to suggest that the creature's foot is flat because an arch would not be able to support the 800-pound weight of an eight-foot tall body. Also, the same size of four smaller toes is typical of many of the casts of the western Bigfoot in the possession of Krantz.

CHAPTER 8

Frequently Asked Questions

I have given presentations about the Pennsylvania Bigfoot over the years, and the audiences frequently ask me the same questions about the creature. I've found it convenient to discuss most of its characteristics by answering the FAQs presented below. Be aware that this information is acquired second-hand via eyewitness testimony.

How tall is the Pennsylvania Bigfoot?

The creature is normally described as being between seven and nine feet tall. The average is seven-and-a-half feet. On occasion, there are reports of heights as low as four feet and as high as 15 feet.

How long is the creature's hair?

Most witnesses pay little attention to hair length, but when they do, it is usually described as being "very long." The lengths vary from four to six inches. The hair is reported as being "very shiny" as often as it is described as being "shaggy and matted."

What is the usual color of the creature's hair?

It is normally described as being brown or black. In parentheses are the numbers of cases in our files that correspond to the given color: dark brown/black (96); brown (38); reddish-brown (15); grey (12); white (4); red (5); orange (1).

What does its face look like?

Most of our sightings are too distant, or it's too dark for facial features to be determined. When reported, witnesses usually describe the face as being more apelike than human. (There are a number of exceptions; note the Sleepy Hollow creature described in Chapter 1). The facial skin is black and is either partially or completely covered with hair. The darkness of the skin prevents witnesses from discerning other features, such as the nose, mouth or ears. When observed, the nose and ears are often described as "close to the face or head" or "not being very prominent."

What is the size and shape of the head?

The creature's head is described as being human-like, but larger. However, witnesses claim the size of the head is what they would expect, considering the extreme height and weight of the animal. A sagittal crest (a ridge of bone running lengthwise along the midline of the top of the skull) and a large brow ridge are sometimes, but not often, reported.

What color are its eyes?

Eyeshine is typically not reported. However, whenever it is, red predominates: red or orange-red (35); orange (13); green (8); yellow (5); white (3); blue-green (1). Eyeshine predominates in the earlier sightings (1970s) of the three- and four-toed creature.

Does it have a neck?

The creature is described as having either a small neck or none at all. Much like a gorilla, Bigfoot can't turn its head very far because its chin comes into contact with its shoulders. Therefore, most witnesses claim the creature "turns at the waist" whenever it wants to look to its side.

How do witnesses describe the shoulders and arms?

The shoulders are broad, and the arms so long that its hands come down to its knees. Occasionally, arms dangling below the knees are observed.

What is the overall description of the features and the movement of the creature?

It is completely bipedal and erect-walking, but it is sometimes described as having bad posture. A typical comment is that it is "slightly stooped at the shoulders." It walks quickly with long strides. Seldom is it ever observed running. As many witnesses state, "it seems to somehow move faster than a human that size would move." It apparently swings its arms more than a human does under normal walking conditions. Under good circumstances, witnesses note that the creature walks with its legs always bent. Grover Krantz discusses this "bent-knee support" with respect to the Patterson film in his book. The bent knee is about 30 degrees of flexion and enables the creature to avoid jarring its body when walking. It has to extend its leg farther than a human with each step to maintain this flexion angle. This may account for the long stride observed in footprint finds.

Is there an odor associated with the sightings?

Usually not, but when it is, the odor is described as sulfur-like or resembling rotten or decaying meat. Another word witnesses commonly use is "musty."

How are the vocalizations described?

When at a distance of several hundred or more yards, witnesses describe a shrill, high-pitched screeching or screaming sound. When the creature is within several feet, witnesses usually hear low-pitched grunts and growls.

Is the Pennsylvania Bigfoot a nocturnal creature?

Of the cases in our files, 52 percent were nocturnal or at dusk, while 48 percent were at dawn or during the daylight hours.

How smart is Bigfoot?

According to Grover Krantz, what distinguishes we humans from apes is our ability to speak, to use tools and to organize into family social groups. His western US Bigfoot demonstrates no ability to do any of these, so he concluded that Sasquatch has an intelligence equal to an ape. I have no evidence to the contrary for the Eastern US Bigfoot in Pennsylvania. Our files have no sightings of a creature using a tool, and we have only four reports of a possible Bigfoot family comprising a father, a mother and a child.

Reality, not imagination

There is no doubt the Pennsylvania Bigfoot is real. The sightings are not figments of witnesses' imaginations, nor are they hoaxes. They are not misidentifications of other animals, such as the black bear. The reality of Bigfoot is verified by hundreds of sightings reported by credible witnesses, and in some cases, supported by physical evidence, such as those very large footprints.

So what is the Pennsylvania Bigfoot? These encounters with grotesque entities appear to be nonsensical, with no purpose except to frighten and confuse, to mystify and confound. Is it a classical animal living in the woods with deer, bobcats and bears? The large majority of Sasquatch investigators think so. It's called the "ape-in-the-woods" hypothesis.

After 40 years of investigating hundreds of these reports in Pennsylvania, I was forced to conclude that the creature is not a "flesh and blood" animal that continually resides and remains hidden in the woods. Its properties violate all of the rules of classical physics.

For example:

- A bear can be tracked through the woods; Bigfoot cannot be tracked.

- At least 4,000 bear are harvested each year in the Keystone State; Bigfoot has been shot at with little effect.

- Bear have been found dead due to natural causes, but no one has ever located a dead Bigfoot.

- Around 300 bear are killed each year in Pennsylvania by vehicular traffic, but there are no reported Bigfoot road kills.

For a variety of reasons, most anthropologists maintain that Sasquatch does not exist.

For example:

- Such an immense creature cannot be eating enough food to survive, because the impact on the food chain would be incredible. This would be apparent to any Pennsylvania game warden.

- There is no fossil record of a large mammal resembling Sasquatch in North America.

- For Bigfoot to be a zoological possibility, thousands need to breed. Why can't we find a dead one?

There exists a small subset of creature reports that can be described only as spooky.

However, I decided that the rules of the quantum world might be used to explain these also. Here are some of the characteristics that fit:

- Appears to be transparent
- Appears to float
- Can move instantaneously from one place to a distant place
- Is not present, then appears instantaneously
- Dematerializes in a flash of light
- Is observed walking in the snow, but leaves no footprints
- Can be tracked for a certain distance, then the tracks suddenly vanish
- Can disappear into an embankment
- Appears impervious to bullets
- Appears to be only partially in our physical world. Is invisible, but the witness hears heavy footfalls and strongly feels its presence
- Is associated with mysterious lights in the sky and on the ground

One fall morning several years ago, I was teaching organic chemistry to about 150 students in a large lecture hall, as I had done for years. Organic molecules are those that contain carbon as one of various elements. The chemical reactions of these molecules involve the movement of particles called electrons. Electrons, protons and neutrons are very, very small subatomic particles that do not obey the laws of classical physics. Instead, they have their own set of rules embedded in a field called quantum physics. Although quantum rules are very strange, and not well understood at the empirical level, they are accepted by physicists and used successfully to predict many phenomena. Understanding quantum rules requires an advanced knowledge of calculus beyond most casual readers.

As I was telling my students about the quantum properties of electrons, it occurred to me that there were some similarities to the properties of Bigfoot. For example, electrons can be a particle and have mass, yet at other times be a massless energy wave. Bigfoot can have mass and leave footprints, but also walk across a snow-covered field and leave no footprints. This prompted me to look at quantum stuff more closely.

CHAPTER 9

Does the Pennsylvania Bigfoot Mimic
the Quantum World?

Once upon a time, about 100 years ago, all was intuitively comfortable with respect to understanding the physical world in mainstream America. There were no flying saucers, Bigfoot or crop circles. Everything obeyed Sir Isaac Newton's three Laws of Motion. Objects were always real and tangible. If a deer ran through the woods, it was possible to measure both the momentum and position of the deer at any time using simple mathematical formulas. An observer looking at or taking a picture of the deer had no effect on the animal's momentum. The running animal wasn't a deer at one moment, then a bear several seconds later. Everything in the world was determinable and predictable. Space and time were absolute.

Then in the early 1900s, along came a group of physicists with names such as Einstein, Planck, Bohr, DeBroglie, Heisenberg and Schrodinger. With theories such as general relativity, special relativity, matter waves and quantum mechanics, they chipped away at the comfortable world of Newtonian physics. Suddenly, the universe operated in mysterious ways. The time on the clock at the railroad station read by a passenger on a moving train was no longer absolute. The time now depended on the speed of the train! Events were now uncertain. They depended on probability, not certainty. Nothing was continuous anymore. Events became discontinuous, i.e., quantized, and the quantum world was born.

If quantum stuff is so weird and bizarre, why is it important, and how do we really know it exists? The answer is embedded in the mathematics. Scientists apply this unusual behavior mathematically using what is called quantum mechanics. It permits us to explain certain phenomena that could not exist if it were not for quantum properties. The mathematics of quantum mechanics enables scientists to accurately predict the behavior of everything from chemical bonds (the glue that holds molecules together) to tiny particles, such as quarks.

One example is nuclear fusion, the process that produces the light and heat in our sun. Using mathematics well beyond the scope of this manuscript, it can be shown that quantum uncertainty permits the nuclei of hydrogen atoms to come close enough to other nuclei so they can interact and combine (fuse) with one another. The rules of classical physics would not permit this to happen. Therefore, if quantum physics were not real, the sun wouldn't shine. If electrons and photons obeyed the laws of classical physics, the laser would not work. DVDs and CDs would not exist. The transistor would not work, i.e., no computers, no email. The MRI would not exist as a diagnostic tool for physicians.

Rule #1: Observation determines reality

The properties of the quantum world are simply bizarre. As noted previously, one of the tenets of quantum theory is that matter is both wave-like and particle-like at the same time. Matter is said to possess wave-particle duality. If a scientist sets up an experiment to show that an electron is a particle, it will appear as a particle. However, if he or she designs an experiment to show that an electron is an energy wave with no mass, it will behave as a wave. This has been verified over and over again in the laboratory. What is the quantum world of small particles really like? Science really doesn't know.

Niels Bohr was a Danish physicist who first developed the theoretical model of the hydrogen atom. He was later to champion what has become known as the Copenhagen interpretation of quantum physics. According to Bohr, the quantum world cannot be described in words. It is simply a collection of probabilities that becomes real whenever an observation takes place. Without an observer, nothing is real. Most physicists adhere to this interpretation.

Another quantum property is called the Heisenberg Uncertainty Principle, which states that it is impossible to determine both the position and momentum of a subatomic particle at the same time. A subatomic particle is just a probability. It doesn't know where it is (position) or where it's going (momentum) until it is observed.

The Heisenberg Uncertainty Principle potentially explains why Bigfoot cannot be captured, tracked or killed, and has no effect on the food chain. By mimicking this quantum rule, the creature does not exist until there is a sighting. If the creature is reported in someone's backyard, it is not observed entering or leaving the area by other local residents. It just "pops into existence." It is not unusual for witnesses to exclaim, "All of a sudden, the creature was there!"

Recall Sam Sherry's encounter in Sleepy Hollow: Sam shined his flashlight toward the area and saw glowing orange eyes, but little else. Suddenly, at the edge of the woods, about 20 feet away, appeared a tall, bipedal creature. Sam was shocked because he did not see the figure walk from the woods to where it stood. It was just suddenly there. This wave-particle duality might also explain the more bizarre encounters, in which the creature is reported to float or glide, or appears to be transparent, as if it had no mass. Or, its footprints suddenly appear. Here are a few examples:

- In Trafford, on 22 September 1980, two boys saw a tall, hairy figure move slowly down a path toward them. It appeared to float or glide rather than walk. Although the body had shiny black hair, the face was human-looking.

- A man and woman were driving at night when their headlights beamed on a seven-foot tall, hairy figure on the road, about 60 yards away. It had shaggy, reddish-brown hair over the entire body. It stood erect, with the head and shoulders slumped, and appeared to glide rather than walk. It disappeared into a ravine. The witnesses also reported seeing a strange nocturnal light in the area.

- In 2000, the Pennsylvania Bigfoot Society received a report from Bradford County in eastern Pennsylvania. A teenage boy, who was mowing his lawn, observed an eight-foot tall, hairy creature float into a wooded area.

- In March 1975, Joan Jeffers investigated a case in which two women observed a creature while driving on South Montour Road near Pittsburgh's North Park. It was seven feet tall and disappeared by simply walking "into" an embankment. This is unacceptable, according to a law in classical physics: "two masses cannot occupy the same space at the same time." Bigfoot and the dirt composing the embankment cannot occupy the same space. However, in the quantum world, things can also be wavelike and have no mass. If the creature was just massless energy, then the women's observation appears reasonable.

- After a creature sighting in February 1994, a series of footprints were found in the snow along railroad tracks in Washington County. Then they instantaneously vanished.

- The creature appears to be impervious to bullets. Some of these cases involved the presence of mysterious lights near the ground or in the sky.

- Near Apollo, Pennsylvania, a tall, hairy creature came out of the woods and walked toward a trailer. Two men shot at it with no visible effect. The creature ran back into the woods and disappeared.

- Sam Frew heard the growling sounds of an animal. He saw something tall with red eyes at a distance in the bushes. He shot at it three times with a rifle, with no apparent effect.

- A man returned home one night to find his dog hung by its neck and his home illuminated by a mysterious light. The witness then saw an eight-foot tall, hairy biped with red eyes. He shot at the creature, but the bullets bounced off with no effect. The creature screamed and ran away.

Rule #2: Quantum states are discrete

Several years ago, a monkey escaped from the Pittsburgh Zoo and headed west. Within hours, residents observed the monkey moving from backyard to backyard and crossing roads. Dozens of sightings of the animal occurred as it migrated through Beaver County into Ohio. Why? Because the monkey must conform to Newton's Laws of Physics. If I hold a ball over my head (high energy level), and then release it, the ball has a natural tendency to fall to the floor (lower energy level). After I release it, the ball must pass my shoulders, then my hips and then my knees, before ultimately arriving at the floor. Again, this is classical physics. An electron at a high energy level will naturally emit energy and fall to a lower energy level.

However, the behavior of subatomic particles is quite different. The electron in the diagram does move from the higher energy level to

Classical World

Quantum World

ball

upper state	●		upper state	electron ●

lower state			lower state	

- -

The ball now falls to the lower state | The electron now falls to the lower state

upper state | upper state

As the ball falls, it passes through the space between the upper and lower states.

The electron moves from the upper state to the lower state, but never appears in between the two.

ball

lower state ● | lower state electron ●

the lower energy level, but it does so by vanishing from one state and then suddenly reappearing at the lower level. Physicists often refer to this as a quantum leap. This fact is easily determined by using instruments available in most physics laboratories. Like the ball in the diagram, the monkey traveling from Pennsylvania to Ohio was required to obey the laws of classical physics. It was observed at various locations between the zoo and where it eventually was recaptured.

Bigfoot sightings, however, are quite different:

- Recall Sam Sherry's encounter in 1988. At the edge of the woods, about 20 feet away from him, appeared a tall, bipedal creature. Sam was shocked because he did not see the figure walk from the woods to where it stood. It was just suddenly there. Then Sam turned his back to the creature and calmly walked to the front door of his car. Suddenly, the creature was there next to him. He didn't hear any footfalls, giving him the impression that it moved much too fast to have walked or run.

- A family in Eastern Ohio was picnicking when they saw a tall, hairy creature standing at the edge of the woods. It suddenly vanished and appeared instantaneously 20 yards away.

Rule #3: Quantum particles are entangled

Two very small particles are somehow virtually intertwined. Quantum mechanics predicts things that simply don't make sense in the classical world. For example, in certain instances, changing the properties of a particle in one place instantly alters the properties of another particle even if it's on the other side of the universe. The phenomenon is referred to as "entanglement." This "faster than light" phenomenon violates the laws of classical physics. However, it was ultimately tested and verified by a physicist named John Clausner. He sent two polarized photons off in opposite directions. When he changed the polarization of one of the photons, the other one instantaneously changed. The two photons

QUANTUMENTANGLEMENT

To a physicist, atoms and molecules are macroscopic particles and obey the laws of classical physics. Imagine a neutral mixture below that is made up of equal amounts of a positively charged particle and a negatively charged particle. If the +/- substance is passed through an electric field, it separates into its two particles. Let's pretend that the negative one is moved to the other side of the universe. If the + one that stayed home is changed to a negative on purpose by the person doing the experiment, it has no effect on the negative one on the other side of the universe.

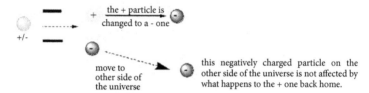

However, if the green ball above is not a molecule or something else big and macroscopic, but instead, is what physicists call microscopic, then something strange happens. Examples of microscopic particles would be things like electrons and photons. When the + particle at home is purposely changed to a negative one, the negative one on the other side of the universe <u>instantaneously</u> becomes positive. It follows the rules of quantum physics. Both must always have opposite charges.

This property is called **"Entanglement."**

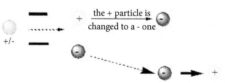

the negative particle on the other side of the universe automatically becomes positive, once the + one back home is changed to a negative one.

remained connected in some mysterious way. It appears as if the quantum world is psychic.

In the Quantum Entanglement box, my purpose is to provide the reader with a flavor of that is this quantum characteristic. In fact, this is how physicists decide whether a particle is classical or quantum. If it exhibits the property of entanglement, then it is assumed to be quantum.

It was once thought that an atom is too large (macroscopic) to undergo entanglement. Only the small subatomic particles such as electrons and protons that make up the atom undergo entanglement, i.e., display quantum effects. Right? I thought so, too, until I noticed a news item in an issue of *New Scientist*. The article reads, "The quantum world is about to get bigger." It goes on to relate an experiment to be performed by physicists that may "allow objects big enough to be seen with the naked eye (macroscopic) to exist in two places at once." Of course, they are talking about "entanglement," which only occurs in the quantum world.

In another experiment, published in a 2001 issue of *Nature*, three physicists from Denmark sent a pulse of light through two gas samples of the element cesium. This resulted in a measurable entanglement for a fraction of a second. Physicists are interested in these types of experiments because of possible applications toward quantum computing.

Physicists are still in the early stages of understanding "entanglement." Scientists are now suggesting that "consciousness" is somehow related to entangled particles in the brain. I suppose that is no surprise since consciousness (awareness) is what makes a person an observer, which in turn permits a probability wave of a quantum electron to collapse and become a particle.

Researchers are now attempting to relate quantum entanglement to psychic phenomena (psi). The phone rings, and one instantaneously knows who is calling. Another example is a loved one is in an accident thousands of miles away, and one instantaneously knows something bad happened to that person. Recall the Bell Township creature case in which Sam Frew sensed that something was following him just before the creature appeared. This feeling that Bigfoot witnesses had that they were being watched occurred in many cases I investigated over the years.

Our data also suggests that anyone having one creature sighting has a much greater chance of having a second or third encounter. In the UFO and Bigfoot fields we refer to these people as being "encounter-prone," and, it is quite common. Sam Sherry saw the creature twice; the birdman had three or four sightings; Bob France had multiple encounters, and so on. Perhaps something in their unconscious minds permits entanglement with Bigfoot. Of course, the creature would have to be in a quantum state for this to occur.

It became apparent to me that the mysterious creature responsible for our Pennsylvania Bigfoot reports is not an "ape in the woods." Instead, it evolves from an alternate reality and conforms to the rules of what we know as the quantum world. Initially, I considered the possibility that the creatures may be visitors from a planet in our galactic neighborhood, or perhaps from other galaxies.

Conjecture about advanced civilizations is a matter of sheer speculation, but I decided to utilize the laws of physics to place upper and lower limits on these civilizations. One method of estimating the technological advancement of an extraterrestrial civilization is to apply the hypothetical scale proposed by Soviet astronomer Nikolai Kardashev. It is based on the amount of energy a specific civilization is able to use:

- Type I Civilization: harnesses all the energy available from its home planet.

- Type II Civilization: harnesses all the energy available from its sun.

- Type III Civilization: harnesses all the energy available from its galaxy. This civilization would be technologically ahead of the earth by at least 100,000 years.

String theory

How can I use these quantum properties to develop an understanding of Bigfoot phenomena in Pennsylvania? Physicists were faced with the same dilemma in their attempts to unite the forces of nature so they could make sense of how the universe operates.

There are four fundamental forces of nature:

1. Electromagnetism (described by Maxwell's equations)

2. Strong nuclear force (holds the nuclei of atoms together)

3. Weak nuclear force (responsible for radioactive decay)

4. Gravity (as described by Einstein's theory of relativity)

In the 1960s-1970s, physicists were able to combine the first three forces because each one has a quantum property. But gravity arises from the classical physics of large objects and is not compatible with the algebraic equations of the quantum world. However, along came "string theory" in the 1990s. The mathematics of string theory generates a quantum particle, called a graviton, for gravity. This unites all four fundamental forces into one coherent framework. In other words, physicists used string theory to unite something very large that conformed to the laws of classical physics, i.e., gravity, with the very small quantum forces.

I asked myself this question: Can I take a very large animal, i.e., Bigfoot, which appears to mimic quantum physics, and in turn use string theory to explain its existence in the classical world?

String theory is a highly complicated, mathematical approach for unifying all the forces of nature. Born in the 1960s, string theory was slowly abandoned by most physicists for 20 years before being reborn in the 1990s. It proposes that the subatomic, quantum particles composing matter are not tiny dots or points. Instead, particles are manifested by smaller vibrating energy filaments, each one described by a complex mathematical equation. A string may be pictured as a tiny, vibrating elastic band, as shown below:

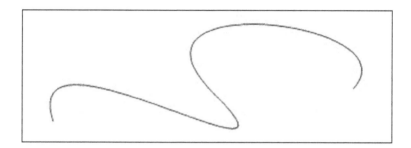

The bands vibrate differently, like the different notes one can play on a banjo. The strings of a banjo are stretched under tension to produce a note. The string also has tension, but it is floating in spacetime. One vibration (note) generates a mathematical expression. The oscillations of these strings provide subatomic particles with their charge, their mass, their spin and so on.

String theory requires the existence of parallel universes, each one having 10 dimensions

There were several formulations of string theory that ultimately evolved into what is called "M-theory." It is considered to be the primary contender for predicting what physicists call the Theory of Everything (TOE). The theory contained not only algebraic equations for handling one-dimensional strings but also equations for handling two-dimensional objects called "branes" (short for membranes). The 2-D brane can also vibrate like a 1-D string. Noted physicist Brian Greene describes it as an undulating "flying carpet."

M-theory also supports the existence of branes that are 3-D, 4-D, etc. However, the mathematics require each one to have 10 dimensions.

The branes can expand and become their own 10-D universe. This leads to the multiverse (parallel universes) theory. Some of these universes can contain galaxies, stars and planets, as ours does. Perhaps our universe is a 3-D brane, and we are embedded within a much larger 9-D space. Because of this, we are not able to observe those other dimensions.

String theory permits the existence of traversable wormholes

As a string moves in time, it warps the surrounding space, generating wormholes. A wormhole is a hypothetical, interdimensional portal or vortex. It acts as a tunnel that may also potentially connect parallel universes. At this point, wormholes exist in theory only but are mathematically supported by several sources.

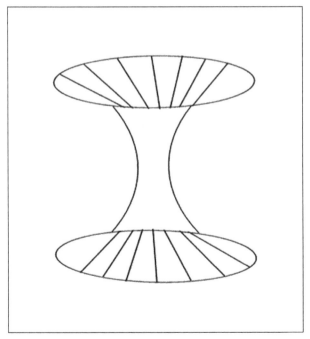

Wormhole

The possible existence of wormholes was proposed by Albert Einstein and his student, Nathan Page, in 1935. A solution to string theory known as the Einstein-Rosen Bridge is also supported by Einstein's general theory of relativity. Maintaining an open, traversable wormhole requires a huge quantity of energy.

Entities of a Type III civilization in another dimension or universe may possess this exotic matter. This would permit them to generate a traversable wormhole and visit us. From our point of view, this would appear as a paranormal event.

Appendix

Partial Chronology of Pennsylvania Creature Reports, 1977-1996

Case 3830

Date: April 1977
Time: Near dusk
Location: Cadogan, Armstrong County

A resident observed a tall, hairy, bipedal creature walking in the woods behind his house.

Case 3840

Date: Early spring 1977
Time: Daylight
Location: Grays Landing, Fayette County
Lat/Long: 39°49'50", 79°55'00"

A man sleeping in his vehicle awoke to an unpleasant odor. Through his rear window he saw a hairy, bipedal creature about 10 feet away. It was almost completely covered with reddish-brown hair and stood between eight and nine feet in height. It was very muscular with broad shoulders and stood perfectly erect. The creature turned and looked at the witness, but there was so much hair on its face he could easily see only the eyes. They were huge, slightly elongated and blinking. The witness started his car and vacated the area. Through the rearview mirror, he observed the creature run away with an unusual stiff-legged gait, unlike the way humans run. Despite this, it was able to run very fast.

Case 3850

Date: 15 May 1977
Time: 9:35 PM
Location: Footedale, Fayette County
Lat/Long: 39°53'55", 79°51'02"

A man and a woman were driving when in their headlight beams they saw a seven-foot tall, hairy figure on the road about 60 yards away. It had shaggy, reddish-brown hair over the entire body. It was erect with the head and shoulders slumped, and appeared to glide rather than walk. It disappeared into a ravine. The witnesses also reported seeing a strange nocturnal light in the area.

Case 3870

Date: 15 June 1977
Time: 3 AM
Location: Glenshaw-Allison Park, Allegheny County
Lat/Long: 40°32'25", 79°57'10"

Looking out a closed window, a college student observed a hairy creature on its knees drinking water from the student's above-ground swimming pool. The creature cupped its hands and brought the water slowly to its mouth. A spotlight illuminated the area. The witness tapped on the window, and the strange figure rose. It was nearly eight feet tall and had long, black hair. It walked into the woods and began breaking branches while making strange "grunting" and "squealing" noises.

Case 3910

Date: July 1977
Time: Daylight
Location: Cadogan, Armstrong County

A man saw a hairy, bipedal creature at a distance in the woods behind his house. It was too far away to discern any detail except for the general shape.

Case 3940

Date: 5 September 1977
Time: Near dusk
Location: Cadogan, Armstrong County
Lat/Long: 40°45'46", 79°38'10"

The witness from the previous sighting was mowing his lawn near dusk when he had a feeling he was being watched. He looked 30 feet into the woods and observed an eight-foot tall figure covered with brown hair. It had a cone-shaped head, broad shoulders and no neck. It appeared to be slightly stooped at the shoulders and was able to hunch down as it moved away from him through the pine trees. He also detected a sulfur odor.

Case 3950

Date: 10 September 1977
Time: Near dusk
Location: Cadogan, Armstrong County
Lat/Long: 40°45'46", 79°38'10"

The witness from the previous case again saw the creature from a distance in the woods behind his house.

Case 3960

Date: 17 September 1977
Time: Daylight
Location: Cadogan, Armstrong County

A man observed a gray-colored creature that walked on two legs with very long strides. He estimated that the hair was at least three inches long.

Case 4000

Date: 11 October 1977
Time: 6:15 PM
Location: Cadogan, Armstrong County
Lat/Long: 40°47'30", 79°35'40"

Several residents were driving on Dutch Hollow Road when they observed an eight-and-a-half-foot tall figure with knee-length arms standing in a field. It had a cone-shaped head, no neck, broad shoulders and black hair. After a minute, it disappeared into the woods.

Case 4010

Date: October 1977
Time: After dark
Location: Latrobe, Westmoreland County

A man returned home one night to find his dog hung by its neck and his home illuminated by a mysterious light. The witness then saw an eight-foot tall, hairy biped with red eyes. He shot at the creature, but the bullets bounced off with no effect. The creature screamed and ran away.

Case 4070

Date: 23 December 1977
Time: 7:30 PM
Location: Trent, Somerset County
Lat/Long: 39°59'00", 79°14'59"

After watching a UFO drop to treetop level after dark in this rural area, two boys later observed a tall, brown-colored, hairy figure with glowing white eyes. It turned and ran. A bright, white light appeared from the area. They later heard several loud "booms" in the vicinity.

Case 4085

Date: 1977
Time: After dark
Location: Coaltown, Allegheny County

A woman observed a large, hairy biped standing at the bottom of a ladder that was leaning against her home.

Case 4170

Date: April 1978
Time: 3 AM
Location: Hooversville, Somerset County
Lat/Long: 40°9'12", 78°54'12"

A resident of this village reported to the police that he observed a large, hairy biped outside his home. He shot at it with no apparent effect. It disappeared into a clump of bushes.

Case 4210

Date: May 1978
Time: 2:30 AM
Location: Apollo, Armstrong County

A woman observed a tall, hairy creature growling and beating on the window air-conditioner of a neighbor's home. After a minute or so, it ran into the woods and disappeared.

Case 4300

Date: May 1979
Time: After dark
Location: Apollo, Armstrong County

A tall, hairy creature came out of the woods and walked toward a trailer. Two men shot at it with no visible effect. The creature ran back into the woods and disappeared.

Case 4360

Date: 15 August 1979
Time: After dark
Location: White Oak, Allegheny County

Witnesses observed a large, dark-colored figure near their home. It "gave out a blood-chilling scream." At first, their dog barked, but then whimpered and cowered.

Case 4365

Date: 18 August 1979
Time: After dark
Location: White Oak, Allegheny County

A large, hairy creature with red eyes was observed at a distance of 50 yards. Three-toed footprints were discovered later at the entrance to a coal mine.

Case 4380

Date: September 1979
Location: Washington County
Lat/Long: 40°06'01', 80°16'39"

Three residents who live along Deerfield Road near Lagonda were in their backyard when they observed tall, hairy creature emerge from a wooded area and lope across an open area, before disappearing into a cornfield. It was about seven feet tall, slightly stooped at the shoulders and had long arms that hung well below the knees. They saw it only in profile but saw that it had coal-black hair over its entire body. Its strides were much longer than those of a normal human.

Case 4400

Date: November 1979
Time: Daylight
Location: Kingwood, Somerset County

Several young boys were snowmobiling when they observed a huge, hairy biped walk across a distant field.

Case 4440

Date: 1979
Time: After dark

Location: Apollo, Armstrong County

A man pulled into his driveway and saw a huge, black, erect-walking creature leaning against a tree. After a few seconds, it retreated into the woods.

Case 4505

Date: 10 January 1980
Time: After dark
Location: Trafford, Westmoreland County

A group of young boys observed a tall, hairy figure with reddish-brown hair and glowing red eyes. They also detected a "sulfur odor" and a strange, white light in the vicinity. The creature retreated to the woods, where it broke branches and threw stones before disappearing.

Case 4575

Date: 26 June 1980
Time: 11:30 PM
Location: Guffey, Westmoreland County
Lat/Long: 40°18'07", 79°45'10"

Two residents saw a large, hairy biped in their backyard. It was dark and they were unable to obtain a good view, but stated that it ran away quickly and was very coordinated. A horse in the area "was jumping all over the place." They also heard the creature make deep breathing sounds.

Case 4580

Date: 30 June 1980
Time: 10:30 PM
Location: Guffey, Westmoreland County
Lat/Long: 40°18'07", 79°45'10"

One of the witnesses from the previous sighting walked outside and heard the heavy breathing sounds again. Seeing a large, hairy biped at a distance, he grabbed a gun and unsuccessfully tried to follow it through a field.

Case 4600

Date: 18 July 1980
Time: 7:00 PM
Location: Columbia County

A young man watched a tall, hairy biped walk down an abandoned railroad bed toward him. He estimated the creature was seven to eight feet tall, weighed 400 pounds and had long, black hair covering most of its body. It had a large head, flattened nose, large eyes and arms that swung well below the knees. The creature turned and ran into the bushes, at which time a frightened deer ran across the tracks.

Case 4610

Date: 20 July 1980
Time: After dark
Location: Guffey, Westmoreland County

Witnesses first saw a strange blue light hovering in a field, and then observed a tall, hairy creature nearby. It moved quickly and made loud, deep breathing noises as it ran away on two legs.

Case 4630

Date: 18 August 1980
Time: 8:45 AM
Location: Jonestown Mountain, Columbia County

Two brothers were driving to work when they observed a tall, erect-walking creature cross the road in front of them. It had thick, shaggy, brown hair, long legs and a stride three times that of a human. They also heard a weird, high-pitched cry. They examined the area later that evening and found a partial lean-to with grass bedding.

Case 4700

Date: 22 September 1980
Time: Afternoon
Location: Trafford, Westmoreland County
Lat/Long: 40°23'08", 79°45'07"

Two boys saw a tall, hairy figure move slowly down a path toward them. It appeared to float or glide rather than walk. The body had shiny, black hair. The face was human-looking.

Case 4730

Date: October 1980
Time: Daylight
Location: Kingwood, Somerset County

A man was walking about 300 yards from a mine opening when he observed a 10-foot tall, hairy creature weighing about 600 pounds. It made a low-pitched, growling sound. His dog cowered at his feet when the creature came within 25 feet of the witness. He ran to his car and vacated the area.

Case 4750

Date: 22 November 1980
Time: 10:45 AM
Location: Kingwood, Somerset County

Two brothers observed a tall, hairy figure walking at a distance of about 250 yards. The creature had an oblong-shaped head with a pointed crown and no neck. It had very broad shoulders, a narrow waist, long strides and long, shaggy brown hair.

Case 4775

Date: 1980
Time: Daylight
Location: Two miles outside of New Florence, Westmoreland County, Game Farm #42.
Lat/Long: 79°30', 40°20'

Three witnesses were walking along a pipeline right-of-way when about 300 yards away they observed a hairy biped. It was between seven and eight feet tall with dark brown hair.

Case 4880

Date: 18 April 1981
Time: After dark
Location: Bell Township, Westmoreland County, Route 819, one mile from Apollo
Lat/Long: 40°33'43", 79°33'55"

Sam Frew observed a four-foot tall, brown, hairy creature that he estimated weighed 1,500 pounds. It made an "eerie growling, hissing" sound and emitted an odor like "spoiled meat." He shot at the creature with an 8mm rifle while observing it in a flashlight beam.

Case 5040

Date: 12 August 1981
Time: Daylight
Location: Bell Township, Westmoreland County, Route 819, 1 mile from Apollo
Lat/Long: 40°33'46", 79°34'12"

A male witness was taking an afternoon walk in the woods when he felt uneasy, as if he were being watched. Then, 50 feet ahead, he briefly observed a large, two-legged figure cross a gas line road. It was at least 12 feet tall with brown hair covering most of its body. The encounter was too brief for him to recognize more details.

Case 5050

Date: August 1981
Time: Afternoon
Location: Bell Township, Westmoreland County, Route 819, 1 mile from Apollo
Lat/Long: 40°33'38", 79°34'7"

A young boy biking along Route 819 looked to his left and saw, at a distance of 50 yards, the back of a tall, hairy biped as it walked from a pasture into a wooded area.

Case 5080

Date: 31 October 1981
Time: After dark
Location: Lancer Park, near Vandergrift, Westmoreland County
Lat/Long: 40°34'54", 79°34'30"

A woman driving her car stated that her headlights illuminated a hairy creature walking across the neighbors' lawn and down a steep hillside. It was seven to eight feet tall with brownish-black hair over its entire body. The creature had a small neck and moved with well-coordinated strides. After the strange figure disappeared over the hillside, she heard many dogs barking crazily in that vicinity.

Case 5130

Date: December 1981
Time: Dawn
Location: Columbia County, State Game Land #58
Lat/Long: 40°57'13", 76°22'13"

A man noticed a foul smell, like a decaying animal, and then observed a strange, apelike creature sitting on the ground about 50 to 75 yards away. It was covered with long, brown hair that "laid down flat." The cone-shaped head had a large brow ridge like an ape, but the face was flat. Suddenly, the creature stood up on two legs and ran away. It ran slightly hunched over with arms down to its knees. It jerked its arms in an unusual fashion while running. The witness estimated that the creature was at least seven feet tall.

Case 5250

Date: 18 June 1982
Time: Near dusk
Location: Chestnut Ridge, Westmoreland County, near Bear Cave
Lat/Long: 40°22'30", 70°14'

As he was walking, Bob France noticed a strange odor permeating the area. He likened the smell to a "mixture of rotten eggs, spoiled potatoes and urine." Then he observed a tall, hairy creature standing behind a boulder. It just stood there gripping the rock and looking at him. The creature then left the rock and walked toward the startled witness. After coming within 10 feet of where Bob stood, the creature abruptly veered to its left, walked into a thicket of high weeds and disappeared. It was bipedal and covered with dark brown and black hair six to eight inches long. The head was completely covered with hair, but it did appear to have a high, broad forehead. It was too dark in the woods for Bob to distinguish facial features. The arms hung down to the knees and each hand appeared to have five fingers. The creature was "very broad and husky, with shoulders slowly rising to the head area, giving it the appearance of having no neck." Bob thought the creature had "an unusual hitch to its stride." It had a long stride in which the entire body dipped and rose as it swung its arms with each step.

Case 5300

Date: 10 September 1982
Time: Dawn
Location: Truman Boulevard in Franklin Borough, Cambria County
Lat/Long: 40°20'10", 78°52'45"

David Gustkey was driving to work when he observed a seven-foot tall, hairy creature cross the road in front of him. It traversed Truman Boulevard in four steps and walked up a hillside. The witness estimated that the creature weighed about 400 pounds. It had long, black hair and an elongated head, but no neck. Our investigators found no physical evidence in the area.

Case 5320

Date: September 1982
Time: 9 PM
Location: York County, Greenvalley Road, outside of York
Lat/Long: 39°51', 76°27'30"

A man and his wife were returning home after shopping. They were in a rural area near a dump when they saw a creature cross the road about one block ahead. They observed it in their high beams only for a few seconds. They described it as being 10 feet tall, bipedal and completely covered with light brown hair.

Case 5330

Date: 6 October 1982
Time: After dark
Location: Bell Township, Westmoreland County, Route 819, one mile from Apollo
Lat/Long: 40°33'42", 79°33'59"

Ruth Frew was doing her laundry in the basement of her home when she heard a loud vocalization and observed a creature with fiery red eyes peering at her through a window.

Case 5345

Date: 28 October 1982
Time: After dark
Location: Bell Township, Westmoreland County, Route 819, one mile from Apollo
Lat/Long: 40°33'42", 79°33'59"

Sam Frew heard the growling sounds of an animal. He saw something tall with red eyes at a distance in the bushes. He shot at it three times with a rifle with no apparent effect.

Case 5390

Date: Fall 1982
Time: Afternoon
Location: Bell Township, Westmoreland County, one mile from Apollo
Lat/Long: 40°33'22", 79°33'57"

Ruth Frew and her son were walking in the woods when they observed a tall, hairy creature slumped over in a thicket. They slowly backed away and returned home.

Case 5585

Date: 1983
Time: After dark
Location: Chestnut Ridge Road, near Kingston, Westmoreland County
Lat/Long: 40°18'31", 79°19'12"

A woman was burning garbage in her backyard when she looked up and saw a huge, hairy creature standing at a distance. "It had a tall head looking as if it had a stove-top hat on," she said.

Case 5590

Date: Fall 1983
Time: Afternoon
Location: East of the town of Jefferson, Greene County

A group of boys were playing when they heard strange noises in the woods. They investigated and observed a hairy creature rapidly moving away from them. They thought it was a bear, but then they noticed it was not shaped like a bear and it walked on two legs. The boys ran home.

Case 5650

Date: 23 March 1984
Time: Afternoon
Location: Bell Township, Rubright Road, Westmoreland County

A man was driving his car when he observed a four-foot tall, hairy biped at a distance of about 400 yards. It had black hair, no neck and a small head, and was very bulky.

Case 5750

Date: Fall 1984
Time: Dusk
Location: Catawissa Township, near Bloomsburg, Columbia County
Lat/Long: 40°58'53", 76°24'54"

A man was burning trash in his backyard when he heard a large animal crashing down through the woods toward him. Suddenly, a huge, hairy creature walking on two legs emerged. It was completely covered with black hair, including the head, which sat directly on its shoulders. It stood there for several minutes and appeared to sway back and forth. The witness also detected a "foul odor, like an open sewer." Then it "let out a God-awful scream." He said it was so loud it echoed off the mountainside. The witness ran into his house to find his gun, but when he returned the creature had disappeared.

Case 5760

Date: 27 October 1984
Time: Afternoon
Location: Harveyville, Luzerne County

A man and a woman were driving along a country road when they saw a tall, bipedal creature walking near a barn. It was completely covered with black hair. By the time the witnesses stopped and turned around, the creature had disappeared.

Case 5830

Date: August 1985
Time: Afternoon
Location: Lebanon County

A nine-year-old boy was walking up the lane toward his house when a creature with big teeth rose from a cornfield and frightened him. He said it was hairy and taller than his dad, who is six feet, four inches. Credit: Richard McGee.

Case 5850

Date: 7 September 1985
Time: 12:15 AM
Location: North Annville, Lebanon County, near Harrisburg

A man and a woman sitting on a screened porch observed a tall, apelike creature walking along a fence line at a distance of approximately 75 feet. The man said the creature had no neck and its head came to a point on top. Its arms seemed unusually long and swung in unison with the particularly long stride. As the creature passed a dog pen, the one-year-old German Shepherd ran inside and became silent. Credit: Richard McGee.

Case 5860

Date: 14 September 1985
Time: After dark
Location: North Annville, Lebanon County, near Harrisburg

The witnesses in the preceding case heard a series of loud shrieks coming from a wooded hollow behind their house. Two weeks later, 12 large footprints were found in the area. Rain had erased some of the details. The indentations were measured to be 18 inches long. Credit: Richard McGee.

Case 5880

Date: Around 1985
Time: After dark
Location: Armstrong County
Lat/Long: 40°36'45", 79°33'20"

A woman and her 10-year-old son were traveling on Dime Road approaching North Vandergrift when they observed two tall, hairy creatures cross the road in front of their vehicle. They had black hair with a reddish tint and large, red eyes. The creatures continued walking, stepped over the guardrails and disappeared.

Case 5960

Date: 13 December 1986
Time: sunset
Location: Gray Station, railroad tracks, Westmoreland County
Lat/Long: 40°24'35", 79°14'20"

A hunter was walking down the railroad tracks toward his home in a trailer park. Suddenly an object fell at his feet. He thought it was a log. He looked up to see a strange, hairy bipedal creature standing on the railroad bed about 100 yards away. The figure's left arm was lowering to its side, giving the witness the impression that this "thing" had thrown the object, presumably to attract his attention. It was apelike, stood between seven and eight feet tall and had long, black hair. The creature had very broad shoulders. "I was scared at first, but I needed to get by him to go back to my trailer," said the witness. "We must have stared at each other for several minutes." The creature had large, red eyes and a huge head that appeared to sit directly on the broad shoulders. The head came to a point at the top and was completely covered with hair. He noticed that the arms were long, hanging slightly below the knees. After several minutes, the creature turned and walked down the tracks, away from the witness and toward Gray Station. Then it suddenly veered to the left and ran into the woods near Harbridge Run. It took tremendously long strides, and the witness heard the creature breathing heavily, "as if it had asthma." The witness continued to walk down the tracks toward home and noticed an uncomfortable, sulfur odor permeating the area. He turned left into his trailer park.

Case 6015

Date: March or April 1987
Time: Afternoon
Location: Westmoreland County
Lat/Long: 40°06'51", 79°23'28"

A man was driving his van west on the Pennsylvania Turnpike just past the Donegal exit. There was snow on the ground, and he observed an eight-foot tall, bipedal creature run across a field toward the highway. The creature ran up the embankment, hopped over the guardrail and crossed to the other side. Then it ran up another embankment and out of sight. The witness, as well as a man in another vehicle traveling eastbound, pulled over. They found 22-inch long footprints in the snow. Credit: Pennsylvania Bigfoot Society.

Case 6060

Date: August 1987
Time: 11 PM
Location: Jackson Township, Greene County, State Game Lands

Four men from Waynesburg, Pennsylvania were trying to attract raccoons, fox and deer by playing a 25-minute tape of a rabbit distress call. Within minutes they heard the brush rustling as if an animal was approaching. This was followed by a strange vocalization. Neither a growl nor a roar, it was loud and low-pitched, as if it were echoing from deep within the chest. "It sounded like something in agony," reported one of the witnesses. The men approached the area cautiously and found a number of broken branches, three to six inches thick and five to six feet from the ground. It was then they saw two orange-colored eyeballs of an animal standing in briars about 50 yards away. It had a large, hairy face with no prominent nose. The head sat directly on its broad shoulders. It was bipedal and covered with reddish-brown hair. The men were unable to estimate the height because it was partially obscured by the briars. After a few minutes, the strange figure backed away and disappeared into the trees.

Case 6080

Date: 26 November 1987
Time: Daylight
Location: New Texas Road, Plum Borough, Allegheny County

A man was cleaning bricks in the backyard of his home when he looked up and saw an orange-colored, hairy biped standing about 200 feet away. He looked down at his work and when he looked up again it was gone.

Case 6100

Date: 1988
Time: Daylight
Location: Westmoreland County, near Torrance

Railroad workers along Packsaddle Gap saw a tall, hairy apelike creature walk up a steep hillside to the Chestnut Ridge.

Case 6130

Date: 19 March 1988
Time: 12:45 AM
Location: Gray Station, Westmoreland County
Lat/Long: 40°23'47", 79°14'4"

The witness was driving along Tannery Hollow Road near Gray Station. Two deer suddenly ran from his right side into a wooded area to his left. Another deer followed. Then a tall, erect-alking, hairy apelike creature did the same thing. He saw the creature only in profile for a few seconds but was able to discern glowing red eyes. It was from seven to eight feet tall with long, black hair and arms below the knees. The witness stopped, rolled down his windows and noticed a musty odor.

Case 6142

Date: 10 May 1988
Time: 9:00 AM
Location: Ligonier Township, Westmoreland County, near Rector
Lat/Long: 40°11'17", 79°13'57"

A man was walking a black labrador near Jacob Miller Road on a cool, overcast morning. The dog stopped abruptly and stared ahead at a figure partially hidden by grapevines and brush about 70 yards away. "At first I thought it was a large, hairy man," remarked the witness. "He had to weigh between 400 and 600 pounds. I blew my dog whistle, causing this thing to turn sideways and walk away. It was then I realized it was not a man but some other kind of creature. It had the strangest shuffling walk where it didn't raise its legs very high. But even with this strange shuffling gait, it moved very quickly and quietly." The witness further stated that, except for a sparse, blondish patch of hair on its chest, the creature was completely covered with dark brown hair. It stood about seven feet tall and was an erect-walking biped with perhaps slightly stooped shoulders. The head was large and round on top. The creature was too far away for the witness to observe any facial details.

Case 6145

Date: 17 May 1988
Time: 11:30 PM
Location: Sleepy Hollow Causeway, Route 30, Westmoreland County
Lat/Long: 40°17'10", 79°19'12"

Sam Sherry had parked his 1975 Maverick next to the Sleepy Hollow causeway and was removing fishing equipment from the trunk when he noticed a musty odor and heard strange noises coming from a wooded area below the eastbound lane of Route 30. "I heard this loud commotion," he said. "There were shrill whistling, grunting and monkey-like chattering sounds coming out of the woods." Suddenly, at the edge of the woods about 20 feet away, appeared a tall bipedal creature. Sam estimated that the strange figure was one or two inches shy of being seven feet tall. The head was larger than a soccer ball but smaller than a basketball. The two eyes were the size of golf balls and exhibited orange eyeshine. The face was "deeply wrinkled and had a leather-like appearance." The facial skin seemed to have a reddish-brown tone as did the rest of the body. The top of the head was bare except for a two-inch high, two-inch wide swath of hair that began at the top of the forehead and extended to the lower back of the head. On each side of the head was a horseshoe-shaped segment of hair that originated below the ears and terminated below the eyes. The creature had no neck. The shoulders were broad and the remaining torso long and indistinct. Each foot had five toes. The creature's arms were long, hanging nearly down to the ankles while standing erect. It had two very large hands, each with four fingers and an opposable thumb. The fingers did not appear to have any claws or nails. There was no hair on the arms, hands, legs, feet or torso. The reddish-brown skin was leathery and well worn. "It was as if this thing was always scratching itself and that's why the skin and fingernails were so worn," said the witness. Areas on the shoulders, elbows and knees were especially deteriorated. There were also a number of gray patches of skin on the knees and torso, as if the creature had a mange-like skin disease.

Sam guessed this creature was very, very old. When initially observed, the creature "stood perfectly erect" with its arms at its side. It was not bent at its shoulders or hips. The witness noticed it was breathing loudly and heavily, as if it had an asthmatic condition. It continually spit saliva as it wheezed. Its mouth was puckered, an effect the witness thought was due to the creature's unusual breathing pattern. According to Sam, it "appeared to suck in more air than it breathed out." Then it finally expelled the pent-up gas in one heavy, long exhalation. The creature began acting in a challenging-like manner. It swung its arms, beat its chest and flexed its muscles. Sam suspected other creatures were still in the woods, and that this one was putting on a display in defense of them. After several minutes, the creature discontinued the display.

Sam turned his back to the creature and calmly walked to the front door of his Maverick. Suddenly, it was there next to him. He didn't hear any footfalls. He had the impression it moved much too fast to have merely walked or run. The creature brushed up against the witness' elbow and fingered his jacket. Sam climbed into his car and closed the door. The windows were down, and the creature put his hands on the opening. "The pressure of its weight pressed the car down," said Sam. "So, I said, 'Listen, Biggie, you're going to bust my tires if you don't stop that.' It leaned its head through the open window and spit all over me as it wheezed." Sam said it had "terrible breath odor" that he likened to "spoiled seafood." "Its head was only two feet from mine, and he slobbered all over my face. I didn't try to wipe the spit off. I was afraid to touch it." Sam started the car and drove away. As he did so, he noticed that creature had not moved. It stood there with its right arm stretched out as if to say goodbye.

Case 6150

Date: 1988
Time: After dark
Location: Elk State Forest, Cameron County, near Sinnemahoning
Lat/Long: 41°20'30", 79°03'

A man saw a creature walking in the woods at a distance of about 200 yards. He observed it only for a few seconds, but noticed it was covered with dark hair and its arms hung below its knees. It walked hunched over at the upper back in a loping manner.

Case 6165

Date: July 1988
Time: Daylight
Location: Ligonier Township, Westmoreland County, two miles east of Laughlintown, on Route 30

The witness was walking his dog in the woods when he heard a shrill scream. Looking up the hill, he saw a huge head covered with so much hair he couldn't see facial features. The creature was crouched in the weeds, so he could only see the hair. The head was three times the size of a human head. The creature walked farther up the hill into the woods and disappeared.

Case 6173

Date: September 1988
Time: 8:30 AM
Location: Derry, Westmoreland County

The witness drove past a neighbor's house on Ruby St. and saw an eight-foot tall, hairy creature standing by a tree outside the bedroom window. The witness pulled into her driveway and parked. When she looked back, the figure had disappeared.

Case 6184

Date: December 1988
Time: Daylight
Location: Point Marion, Fayette County

A woman saw a large, dark hairy creature near her home. It was at least seven feet tall.

Case 6186

Date: December 1988
Time: After dark
Location: Point Marion, Fayette County

The mother of the previous witness also saw a large hairy creature near her home. It had long arms that fell below its knees.

Case 6190

Date: 12 December 1988
Time: 10 AM
Location: Gray Station, Westmoreland County
Lat/Long: 40°24'25", 79°14'20"

Two hunters were in a field near Gray Station, less than one mile west of the railroad tracks. The temperature was 12 degrees F. and there was snow on the ground. One hunter saw movement at a distance and drew his friend's attention to it. Upon raising his rifle and looking through the scope, the second man saw an apelike creature walking along the edge of a wooded area. It was tall with long, black hair over its entire body. The witness could see its breath condensing in front of its face as it walked swiftly toward another wooded area. "Even through the scope I couldn't see much of the face," said the witness. "It was too dark-colored. I could see that it had two large breasts, making me think it was a female." The head was large and "came to a point on the top." They watched the figure continue to walk until it disappeared into an area the locals call the "square woods." The witnesses later found a three-toed print in the snow where the creature had walked.

Case 6195

Date: Late 1988
Time: Near dusk
Location: Game Farm #2, near New Florence, Westmoreland County
Lat/Long: 40°21', 79°03'

The witness and his young daughter were walking in Game Farm #2 about two miles west of New Florence. They saw a seven-foot tall, hairy creature walking in a "bent over posture" about 20 yards away. It was very thin and had brown hair. They did not notice any odor.

Case 6205

Date: January 1989
Time: Dawn
Location: Derry Township, Westmoreland County
Lat/Long: 40°24'40",79°15'46"

The witness was walking in the flood control area along old Route 217 where the village of Cokeville was once located. He looked up and observed a hairy creature walking over a hillside in a loping manner. It was about six feet in height and completely covered with dark brown hair. Its oval-shaped head appeared too large for its body. The face was flat and hairless. It came within 100 feet of the witness and then walked out of sight.

Case 6208

Date: January 1989
Time: Dawn, with fog
Location: Derry Township, Westmoreland County
Lat/Long: 40°20'40",79°17'10"

The witness was driving in Peach Hollow between Derry and Hillside when he first observed a tall figure walking in the woods on two legs. He noticed that it was covered with orange-colored hair but saw no other detail.

Case 6240

Date: 20 May 1989
Time: Dawn
Location: Westmoreland County

The witness was fishing in a stream three miles east of Jennerstown. He was returning to his car when he observed a hairy bipedal creature walking about 50 yards away. It had dark brown hair, an oval-shaped head and no apparent neck. It walked aggressively in a zigzag fashion, apparently trying to avoid brambles. He could hear it grunting and could also hear the heavy footfalls. After about 45 seconds, it disappeared into the woods. It apparently never noticed the witness.

Case 6245

Date: Spring 1989
Time: Daylight
Location: Chestnut Ridge, Westmoreland County

Bob France and his nine-year-old son were camping along Trout Run on the Chestnut Ridge. His son saw an eight-foot tall, hairy biped come from the brush and walk over an embankment. He called his father, who saw only the movement of bushes as the creature ran up a hillside.

Case 6255

Date: August 1989
Time: 7 PM
Location: Stony Creek Twp., Somerset County

A man, woman and two youngsters were riding ATVs on a mountain ridge. As they maneuvered along a power line right-of-way, a tall, hairy bipedal creature walked from the brush about 500 feet ahead to the middle of the road where it abruptly stopped, turned and stared at the witnesses. They estimated that it was about seven-and-a-half feet tall, with six-to-eight-inch long, light brown, straggly hair. It stood "bent over, as if it had bad posture." The arms dangled at its knees. After about five minutes, the creature ran into the brush.

Case 6270

Date: 7 October 1989
Time: 3 PM
Location: Indiana County, near Homer City
Lat/Long: 40°32'33", 79°10'37"

Four men were riding in a car on Route 56 several miles west of Homer City when they observed a hairy, erect-walking biped step from the right side about 35 yards away and in two strides cross the road in front of them. It was at least eight feet tall and completely covered with dark brown hair. The creature's head was round and completely hair-covered. They saw it only in profile. It was slim in stature and was perhaps a "bit bent over" when it walked. It walked in a stiff-armed, stiff-legged manner. The driver parked the car. The men climbed out and ran to where the creature disappeared. They never saw it again.

Case 6330

Date: Spring 1990
Time: After dark
Location: Westmoreland County, near Darlington

A resident looked out his back window and saw a five-foot tall, hairy bipedal creature with glowing red eyes. It made high-pitched screaming noises that caused the witness's horses to run to the opposite end of the pasture. The high-pitched sounds were continually heard throughout the summer, sometimes so loud the windows shook.

Case 6335

Date: March 1990
Time: 11 PM
Location: north of Lock Haven, Lycoming County

Four men from Ohio were camping on Cedar Run. They were in their tents at 11 PM when they heard a "drawn out, loud, screeching yell." They were both stunned and scared, so several crawled from their tents and built a fire. Two of them shined flashlights into the woods where they saw two pairs of yellowish-gold eyes "about the size of pineapple rings." They noticed that the eyes blinked. One pair of eyes was seven feet from the ground; the other pair was 10 feet. They appeared to be the eyes of two shadowy figures that stood on the ground. The witnesses slowly walked toward the figures, but the eyes disappeared, and they heard heavy footfalls of "something running down the hill." As they returned to the campsite, they saw another pair of yellow eyes by their tent. They ran toward the tent while waving their arms and yelling. The creature turned and ran. All four men heard heavy, bipedal footfalls as it ran. In all, they believed they encountered three creatures, two in the woods and one by their tent.

Case 6345

Date: 22 June 1990
Time: 3 to 4 PM
Location: Bald Eagle Township, Clinton County

The witness was driving his pickup truck on Old Schoolhouse Road in Bald Eagle Township. Upon turning only Lusk Road, he saw a tall, hairy creature hop over the guardrail on the right side of the road. The witness slammed on his brakes and stopped within 10 feet of the figure. A car behind him also stopped. He described the biped as being seven to eight feet tall with long, brown, shaggy matted hair, giving the animal a grotesque appearance. The face was hair-covered, but he was able to see the eyes, which he described as almond-shaped and dark in the center but lighter around the outside. The head was large and sat on a short, thick neck. The creature had a muscular build and long arms. Its fingered hands dangled about four feet from the ground. The witness noticed a terrible odor, which he likened to rotten garbage. The creature surveyed the cars and then walked to the opposite side of the road. Emitting a pig-like grunt, it went over the embankment and disappeared into the woods.

Case 6360

Date: Summer 1990
Time: After dark
Location: Washington County

During the summer, several family members saw a nine-foot tall, hairy biped about 100 feet away. The body was covered with long, reddish-brown hair. The face was covered with a lighter brown hair. It had green eyes. It streaked into the woods slapping trees aside with its arms. It stayed in the woods for a while, making high-pitched screaming sounds.

Case 6370

Date: October or November 1990
Time: After dark
Location: Indiana County

A young high school student was asleep in his trailer located in a rural area near Brush Valley. He awoke to a noise on the back porch that was attached to the trailer. He walked to the kitchen, where he peered out the window and saw a hairy apelike creature standing on the porch. It had small toes, brown eyes and a cone-shaped head with a brow ridge. The face had black, wrinkly skin partially covered with hair. It had a small nose flattened against its face. The creature jumped from the porch and ran into the woods.

Case 6440

Date: May 1991
Time: After dark
Location: Clinton County

An elderly couple was driving on Lock Haven Road when they saw some very tall people crossing the road in front of them. As they approached, the witnesses observed three hairy bipedal creatures. They appeared to be a male, female and juvenile. The figures paid no attention to the car, but stepped over a guardrail and disappeared into the woods.

Case 6445

Date: 7 June 1991
Time: Dawn
Location: White Deer Creek Road, Union County

The two witnesses were standing alongside their vehicle when they heard loud noises in the woods. Suddenly a tall, hairy bipedal creature appeared. It stopped about 30 feet away from them and they heard its heavy breathing. The creature put its hands on its hips as if it "were going to strike a pose." Instead, it ran a hand down its hip to the thigh, displaying a five-fingered hand. The creature was about eight feet tall and completely covered with long, stringy brown hair. The eyes were large and black, and the nose did not protrude to a large degree. The figure seemed to move its thin lips as if it wanted to say something, but it never opened its mouth to show any teeth. When the creature stepped toward the witnesses, they hastily climbed into their vehicle. The creature walked down the road away from them, broke into a trot and disappeared into the woods.

Case 6450

Date: June 1991
Time: 1 PM
Location: LaMar Township, Clinton County

A young man and his friend were at Long Run when they heard loud footfalls coming from the woods. Upon looking in that direction, they observed a large hairy creature on two legs. They watched the seven-foot tall figure for several seconds before it disappeared behind some bushes about 30 feet away.

Case 6460

Date: 10 July 1991
Time: Daylight
Location: Washington Township, Westmoreland County
Lat/Long: 40°32'25', 79°37'

The witness observed the head and shoulders of a tall, hairy creature as it walked away from him in the woods behind his home. It had black hair and was about 20 yards away. He later found five-toed, 15-inch-long and six-inch-wide footprints.

Case 6485

Date: 21 September 1991
Time: 9-10 PM
Location: Washington County, near Canonsburg
Lat/Long: 40°16'29", 80°09'15"

The witness observed an eight-foot tall, hairy bipedal creature in the backyard of his home on West McMurray Road. It was about 30 yards away but made no noise when it walked. Its arms swung back and forth below the knees, and the head bobbed up and down. It was exceptionally thin and covered with black hair. It simply faded from view.

Case 6492

Date: Fall 1991
Time: Daylight
Location: Somerset County

While driving her two children to school, a woman rounded a curve in the road near Rockwood and saw a hairy bipedal creature cross the road in front of her. It was taller than her van, and she didn't know how she avoided hitting the beast. Credit: Chestnut Ridge Bigfoot Center.

Case 6515

Date: Early 1992
Time: Daylight
Location: Somerset County

Two boys were riding dirt bikes near the village of Scullton when a tall, hairy creature walked out of the woods. It was about seven-and-a-half feet in height, covered with gray and black hair, and walked upright on two legs.

Case 6520

Date: 30 May 1992
Time: After dark
Location: Derry, Westmoreland County
Lat/Long: 40°19'13", 79°18'07"

For several nights in a row, outside his mobile home in Derry, the witness's dogs barked at something. One evening, he went outside with a rifle to investigate and saw glowing red eyes. They belonged to a tall, hairy creature standing on two legs. The witness felt compelled not to shoot. The mysterious figure turned and walked away.

Case 6530

Date: May 1992
Time: 3 AM
Location: Somerset County

A man was awakened by his dogs barking and observed from his window a nine-foot tall creature. It was covered with shaggy black hair, had very long arms and stood on two legs. He left to turn on his outside lights, and when he returned the figure had disappeared.

Case 6535

Date: Summer 1992
Time: Dusk
Location: Washington County, near Canonsburg
Lat/Long: 40°16'33", 80°08'57"

Three teenagers were walking along railroad tracks that parallel West McMurray Road. At a distance, they saw a tall, hairy creature standing near the trestle over Chartiers Creek. The figure suddenly crawled down the embankment toward the creek.

Case 6540

Date: July 1992
Time: After dark
Location: Washington County, near Canonsburg
Lat/Long: 40°16'28", 80°09'12"

Several young men were standing around in the backyard of a home on West McMurray Road when they noticed five tall creatures with green eyes standing in the neighbor's backyard. One witness estimated that the tallest figure might have been 12 feet in height.

Case 6550

Date: 5-6 August 1992
Time: After dark
Location: Elk County

Three campers heard high-pitched vocalizations. Using a flashlight, one of them saw the legs of a hairy bipedal creature. It had glistening, black hair at least six inches long. One camper tried to take a picture with a flash camera; however, this apparently frightened the creature because it ran uphill, stood on a plateau and started screaming. It sounded as if another creature answered and came down the hill to meet the first one. The vocalizations were loud, high-pitched and drawn out. Several more unsuccessful attempts were made to get a picture. The witnesses were scared, so they climbed into their truck. While there, they saw one tall figure cross in front of them by the campfire. They stayed in the truck for an hour and then left the area.

Case 6553

Date: July or August 1992
Time: 10 PM
Location: Washington County, near Wylandville

A young woman was driving her car when she saw a creature moving on a hillside. She stopped the car as the animal came down and quickly walked across the road. In her headlight beams, she saw that it was from seven to eight feet tall, walking on two legs and covered with dark, shaggy hair. It was apelike and had long arms. Suddenly, another creature, followed by two shorter ones, crossed the road. The witness was frightened and raced away.

Case 6557

Date: August or September 1992
Time: After dark
Location: Washington County, near Canonsburg

Three teenagers were in a yard near Canonsburg when they observed a figure between eight and nine feet tall standing by a tree. It was completely hair-covered and had green eyes. Within a minute, it walked away.

Case 6570

Date: 12 October 1992
Time: 10 AM
Location: Chestnut Ridge, Westmoreland County
Lat/Long: 40°20'34", 79°13'44"

The witness was driving a bulldozer near a fire tower when he saw a creature between seven and eight feet in height cross the road about 150 yards away. It was bipedal and was covered with reddish-brown hair. The creature was running, and the witness observed it for only a second or two. Credit: Chestnut Ridge Bigfoot Center.

Case 6575

Date: 13 October 1992
Time: 3:30 PM
Location: Chestnut Ridge, Westmoreland County
Lat/Long: 40°20'22", 79°13'57"

A mechanic was repairing a bulldozer near the fire tower on the Chestnut Ridge when he saw a hairy biped rushing through the woods. "It made lots of noise," he said. An investigator from the Chestnut Ridge Bigfoot Center examined the area the next day and found it was trampled and a number of trees were broken. Credit: Chestnut Ridge Bigfoot Center.

Case 6590

Date: 29 November 1992
Time: 11 PM
Location: Somerset County

Two witnesses were walking in the woods with rifles when they saw large tracks with long strides in the snow. While one of the witnesses stood by a tree, a tall, hairy creature came up to him and brushed against his cheek. It was about nine feet tall. He saw no other details. The witness became disoriented and his friend helped him out of the woods.

Case 6594

Date: 1 December 1992
Time: Dawn
Location: Indiana County
Lat/Long: 40°29'15", 79°04'30"

A hunter in Brush Valley reported seeing a seven-to-eight feet tall, apelike creature. It was a cold day. The witness had just walked into a wooded area when he noticed an odor resembling "an open sewer." He looked up and saw a figure covered with brownish-black hair running away from him at a distance of 50 yards. He shot at it and then chased the creature over a hillside where it disappeared.

Case 6655

Date: 31 January 1994
Time: After dark
Location: Washington County, near Richeyville

A woman was driving at 45 mph on a rural road near the Centerville-Deem's Park-Richeyville area when a tall, hairy biped came out of the woods and ran alongside her car. The creature stayed with the vehicle for about 100 yards before turning into the woods.

Case 6665

Date: 5 February 1994
Time: 2 PM
Location: Washington County, North Strabane Township
Lat/Long: 40°16'34", 80°08'45"

A woman was looking out her window that faces the Chartiers Creek when she saw a figure walking in a large field about 200 yards away. It was much taller than a human, completely covered with black hair, and walked with tremendously large strides. The head was hair-covered, and the creature appeared to have no neck. She quickly called her son to the window, but he observed only the long, hairy legs as the creature disappeared into the woods. The ground in the field was wet and partially snow-covered, but no prints were found the next day. However, prints were found in the snow beside the railroad tracks along the ridge above the field. They were five-toed, 18 inches long, eight-and-a-half inches wide at mid-foot, with a step distance of 50 inches.

Case 6682

Date: 17 June 1994
Time: 11:45 AM
Location: Camp Bayshore, Lebanon County

Two men were hiking along a stream in the woods near Camp Bayshore when they heard a loud groaning sound. On the cliff above the stream, they saw a hairy bipedal creature pushing a large rock. The creature was about seven-and-a-half feet tall and completely covered with long, brown hair. They were unable to see any facial details. After about 10 seconds, the frightened witnesses ran away.

Case 6685

Date: 29 June 1994
Time: Daylight
Location: Chestnut Ridge, Westmoreland County
Lat/Long: 40°19'41", 79°15'28"

A couple was driving on the Ridge Road during a hailstorm when a tall, hairy biped crossed in front of their car and continued walking down an old logging road. It had long, brown hair. The witnesses were unable to discern any facial features.

Case 6691

Date: 2 October 1994
Time: Near sunset
Location: Pennsylvania Turnpike, Westmoreland County

After spending the day in Pittsburgh, two women headed east on the Pennsylvania Turnpike toward Gettysburg. At about 6 PM, they pulled off the road where a picnic table sitting on a large concrete block permitted them to have a light dinner. They noted that except for the vehicular traffic, it was unusually quiet. Suddenly they heard loud sounds of branches breaking and the footfalls of an animal coming quickly down the mountain. After about a minute, the witnesses observed a tall, hairy bipedal creature arrive at the bottom of the hill about 20 feet away and partially seclude itself behind some bushes. The creature held one hand over its face and glared at them with a menacing expression. The women immediately retreated to their vehicle and quickly drove away on the turnpike. They described the creature as being apelike, bipedal, at least eight feet tall, and covered with long, dark brown hair. They detected no odor, but one of the women noticed that the figure possessed male genitalia. Its hands were large and had five digits. It had a flat nose and a large mouth in which one of the women observed teeth.

Case 6695

Date: December 1994
Time: Daylight
Location: Jefferson County

Several hunters were in the woods near Big Run during buck season. It was raining heavily as they observed two hairy bipeds walking beside the creek about 100 yards away. The larger one had dirty brown hair; the smaller one, which they presumed was female, had gray hair. One of the creatures picked up a log and threw it into the creek.

Case 6705

Date: 7 January 1995
Time: After dark
Location: Washington County, near Canonsburg

A woman was driving to work on Hahn Road when a tall, hairy bipedal creature crossed the road about 100 yards ahead. She saw no details.

Case 6725

Date: 25 June 1995
Time: 3:15 AM
Location: Cambria County, near Ebensburg
Lat/Long: 40°29'55", 78°46'30"

Joe Nemanich and a friend were driving west in a pickup on Route 422. Just after passing through the village of Revloc, the high beams of their headlights illuminated what they first thought was a deer crossing the road. Then the witnesses realized the creature was bipedal and completely covered with dark brown hair. The figure was moving from their right to left and was about in the middle of the two-lane road when they first saw it. It walked into the woods and disappeared. The excited witnesses stopped, turned the vehicle around and shined the headlights into the woods but were unable to see it again. When first observed, the creature was about 100 yards away, so they were unable to observe any facial details. Joe noticed that the figure was broad at the shoulders and narrow at the waist. He also seemed to think the legs were "fuzzy," as if shrouded in a mist, although it was a clear night with no fog.

Case 6775

Date: 14 October 1995
Time: 3 PM
Location: Northumberland County

Three boys were walking up a power line clear-cut toward a field where they intended to play football. Suddenly they heard screaming followed by loud footfalls. Then about 100 yards away a creature stepped from the woods into the clear-cut and continued the high-pitched screaming. It was bipedal, about eight feet tall, and completely covered with long hair. The hair on its head was down to its shoulders, and it appeared to have no neck. Its arms were long but did not hang below the knees. The boys turned and ran.

Case 6810

Date: 22 January 1996
Time: 4:55 PM
Location: Madison Township, Armstrong County
Lat/Long: 40°57'00", 79°30'20"

A state trooper was driving his marked police vehicle on State Road 1004. The temperature was 40 degrees F. and there was snow on the ground. About 20 yards ahead, a tall, hairy bipedal figure stepped out of the woods. It stopped, looked at the approaching vehicle, then continued across the road and disappeared into a thicket of laurel bushes. The entire incident transpired in about 10 seconds. The witness estimated the creature was seven to eight feet in height and weighed about 400 pounds. Except for the area around the mouth, nose and eyes, the figure was completely covered with brown to dark brown hair. The hair on its back was darker than that on its front. He described the hair as being "long, similar to a shaggy dog." He said the shoulders drooped, and it was "barrel-chested." The back of the head was pointed, and it had a "very pronounced forehead." The "nose was flat, the mouth was normal and the lips appeared tight." The eyes were almond-shaped and about the size of a quarter. The trooper was amazed at what he had observed. "I couldn't believe I was actually witnessing this," he said. He pulled his vehicle to side of the road and walked to the area where the creature crossed. There he found a series of footprints in the snow. They were human-like, about 18 inches long and with five toes. He noticed no odors.

Printed in the USA
CPSIA information can be obtained
at www.ICGtesting.com
LVHW011105180923
758463LV00001B/201